# PERSONAL EQUITY PLANS

*HOW TO BUILD UP A NEST-EGG IN SHARES – WITH TAX RELIEF*

John Campbell

## A WOODHEAD-FAULKNER MONEYGUIDE

Woodhead-Faulkner · Cambridge

Published by Woodhead-Faulkner Ltd
Fitzwilliam House, 32 Trumpington Street, Cambridge CB2 1QY, England

First published 1987

**British Library Cataloguing in Publication Data**

Campbell, John
    Personal equity plans: how to build
    up a nest-egg in shares, with tax
    relief. — (A Woodhead-Faulkner money guide).
    1. Investments — Great Britain
    2. Stocks — Great Britain
    I. Title
    332.6'322      HG5432

ISBN 0-85941-419-1

ISBN 0-85941-437-X (cased)

Designed by Jane Norman
Typeset by Goodfellow & Egan, Cambridge
Printed in Great Britain by Biddles Ltd, Guildford and King's Lynn

# Contents

# Preface

Since their introduction at the beginning of 1987, Personal Equity Plans (or PEPs) have come in for widespread criticism. Some of this criticism, especially that relating to the scheme's over-complicated small print, is justified. But much of it merely reflects the lack of enthusiasm felt in many City quarters for a product difficult to manage profitably. Some of it, too, appears to be a manifestation of that 'short-termism' to which the financial world is increasingly prone.

In this book, I hope to demonstrate that PEPs can be much more useful, and to many more people, than is often supposed. Compared with many rival investment vehicles (particularly life assurance contracts), PEPs yield nothing in terms of the tax concessions available, and can often be superior in terms of cost. But their main attraction (after a one- to two-year qualifying period) must be their flexibility. With no contractual obligations, PEP investors are free to contribute as much (up to a £2,400 annual limit) or as little as they please in any one year. They can withdraw their funds tax-free within two years, or leave them to accumulate (still tax free) for decades. They can choose a scheme which concentrates on the income-tax exemption, or one which goes all-out for capital growth. Above all, they can choose how – and to what degree – they want their money managed. People who want professional fund management can secure it at a very moderate cost. Those with the confidence to make their own investment decisions have the freedom to do so – though that freedom, as yet, is seldom absolute. Galling though this may be to investors already active on the market, it does provide some useful guidance for the increasing number of people now ready to make their stock market debut. In any event, as PEP portfolios grow larger (and become more profitable to manage), so the current limitations on freedom of action can be expected to wither rapidly. It is still very early days.

The book is in two parts. The first explains how PEPs work, examines the very different types of scheme currently available, and suggests ways in which PEPs might be used to best advantage. The second is aimed mainly at people who still (unnecessarily) regard the stock market as an unfathomable mystery, and who might appreciate a basic grounding in some aspects of investment. The prime aim of the scheme, after all, is to encourage people to take increasing responsibility for their own investment decisions – to become direct participants in the wealth creation process.

John Campbell
August 1987

# 1. Introduction

When Chancellor Nigel Lawson announced the introduction of Personal Equity Plans in his 1986 Budget, it caused widespread surprise. For years, the Thatcher Government had paid lip service to extending private ownership of wealth; and in terms of house ownership, had scored an important success with its policy of allowing council tenants to buy their own homes. Yet, in this, it was clearly working with the grain – home ownership has been a cherished ideal for the British public for decades.

Attempting to change public attitudes towards share ownership, to encourage the man in the street to take a direct financial interest in British industry, was of an entirely different order of difficulty. For years private investment had been in apparently irreversible decline. The stock market, always politically contentious, was regarded with considerable mistrust by the majority of the population; most people regarded it as a glorified casino for the wealthy, and well-nigh incomprehensible to boot. Nor, in its early years, and despite much prompting, had the Government shown much interest in changing this state of affairs. True, it had removed some of the worst tax disincentives to share ownership. It had also gone out of its way to encourage workers to own shares in their own firms. With the launch of British Telecom in November 1984, it had encouraged over one million people to buy shares for the first time. But what it hadn't done, and what many observers thought it must do if a genuine increase in share ownership were to be achieved, was to offer direct tax incentives for investment on the stock market. For this, there was a well-known precedent – for several years, since the introduction of the *loi Monory*, the French have been allowed to write off a proportion of their equity investment against income tax. Despite pleas from many quarters, the British Government had shown little interest in following suit – so little, in fact, that by 1986 lobbyists on behalf of the private investor had become somewhat discouraged.

Nonetheless, PEPs duly arrived in that year's Budget – and if they don't go as far as the *loi Monory*, and still leave enthusiasts for wider share ownership unsatisfied, there's no doubt that they provide a significant additional motive for investors to take the stock market seriously. Admittedly, this has not often been apparent from much of the press comment which has dogged the scheme virtually from its inception. Critics claim that the tax concessions are hardly worth having, that the scheme is an administrative nightmare, and that other forms of investment retain unbeatable advantages. Most of these comments contain a grain of truth – though it all depends on personal circumstances and investment aims. One of the purposes of this book is to show that PEPs, properly used, can be both an efficient and flexible way of building wealth, with several advantages over alternative homes for savings. Even in its current form, the PEP scheme deserves to succeed in attracting more private investors to the stock market.

Whether, alone, it can achieve the Government's avowed aim of creating a 'share-owning democracy' is debatable, but at least it seems to have made a promising start. At the end of January 1987, after the scheme had been in operation for only a month, a Government survey showed that 60,000 people had invested a total of £110 million in PEPs, and that nearly 150 plan managers had been registered with the Inland Revenue. Two months later, another 20 managers had registered – while the number of PEP investors was estimated to have doubled. However, it is probably unwise to extrapolate too far from these figures. In the early months, inevitably, disproportionate use was made of PEPs by existing equity investors. A true assessment of the scheme's success can only be made once it has ceased to be a novelty.

## THE DECLINE OF THE PRIVATE INVESTOR

Thirty years ago, nearly two-thirds of all British shares were in private hands. By the turn of the 1980s, that figure had halved and was still falling rapidly. When the Conservative Government took office in 1979, only 3 million people (or 7% of the adult population) still had any direct interest in shares, and many of these were elderly. As later generations grew up with no knowledge of the stock market and no experience of share buying, it was almost universally accepted that the private investor was gradually dying out.

The decline of the private investor had many causes. First and foremost, perhaps, he had been made a direct target for assault by the taxman. The introduction of capital gains tax in the mid-1960s restricted one of the main incentives for investing in equities – particularly as it then taxed inflationary as well as real gains. Later, the arrival of the investment income surcharge – a 15% levy on top of the investor's marginal rate of income tax – meant that higher-rate taxpayers were suffering virtual confiscation of dividend income. In these circumstances, private equity investment could not compete effectively with alternatives partially or wholly exempt from these disincentives. Housing, pensions and insurance were all much more tax-efficient – and, as taxes rose, making tax avoidance a national obsession, it was inevitable that savings were increasingly channelled either into the housing market or into the big investment institutions.

Of course, private savings were still ending up on the stock market – insurance companies and pension funds invest a huge proportion of their premium income in UK Government securities (gilts) and shares. Nonetheless, control of these investments was passing inexorably away from individuals into a small number of City-based fund managers. As their power rose, so stockbrokers concentrated more and more on serving the institutions' needs – many of them merging to form much larger organisations capable of supporting a major research effort. In the process (at least in the City), the private investor was regarded as increasingly irrelevant and bothersome. In the 1970s, many smaller clients of City firms were either unceremoniously turfed out, or else encouraged to invest in in-house unit trusts.

Another major factor in the private investor's decline was probably simple loss of confidence. In 1973-74, the stock market suffered a catastrophic reverse – its worst since 1940 – and it is known that many individual investors panicked out in the course of the decline. Having lost money, many people decided that the stock market was too treacherous for the average man, and resolved never to get their fingers burnt again. In the 1970s, as 'corporatism' reached its peak, and economic difficulties mounted, an increasing number of people were persuaded that there was no sensible alternative to entrusting their savings to professionals. The idea that the small man could possibly compete with the 'experts' seemed almost laughable. Even those still willing to invest directly on the stock market increasingly sought the protection of unit trusts.

# THE RENAISSANCE OF SHARE OWNERSHIP

Ten years on, the atmosphere of the late 1970s had changed out of sight. Corporatism had gone out of fashion, and with it the idea that experts necessarily knew best. After the traumatic recession of 1980–81, the economic record was one of steady economic growth – and (for those in work) steadily increasing living standards. The substantial fall in inflation led to greater confidence in the value of financial assets. Above all, the whole period was accompanied by one of the biggest Bull markets in living memory.

Anecdotal evidence would suggest that the private investor started to crawl back into the stock market sometime in 1982–83. Certainly, the circulations of investment magazines started to rise quite fast from that period, while 'tipsheets' (or newsletters devoted to recommending shares) have been proliferating ever since. Of course, many of these investors had previous experience of the stock market, and were merely coming out of retirement. They found that conditions for equity investors had improved slightly. Among the first actions of the new government were the abolition of the investment income surcharge, and the indexing of capital gains tax to allow for inflation. In addition, Nigel Lawson abolished the tax relief on insurance policy premiums in his 1984 Budget, reducing the attraction of this alternative form of investment. Nonetheless, there is little evidence to suggest that genuine 'new' stock market investors were emerging in any numbers.

Without a doubt, the great turning point was the privatisation of British Telecom in November 1984. This was preceded by a massive advertising campaign to attract private investors. The exercise was far more successful than anyone expected – well over two million people applied for shares, more than half of whom had no previous experience of the stock market. Moreover, the demand from the public was so great that the institutions (much to their chagrin) were left short of stock, and were forced to pursue the shares through the market. This, in turn, led to a very rapid and substantial rise in the price, and demonstrated to many that the stock market could indeed be highly profitable.

Only a few stockbrokers in the provinces had used the Telecom launch to try to drum up business. After the event, however, the private investor suddenly swung dramatically back into fashion. With the 'Big Bang' looming, many smaller stockbrokers saw the private investor as a means of salvation – and even big City firms were quick to organise cheap 'no frills' dealing services. Others linked up with provincial brokers, some of which merged to form nationwide stockbroking chains offering a wider range of financial services. Having been ignored for two decades, the private investor now saw his custom being actively wooed. If, at the beginning of 1987, this unprecedented promotion of stockbroking services waned rapidly, it was only because the demand was putting many firms' administration under severe strain.

Since Telecom, of course, there have been several other privatisations – notably British Gas, British Airways, Rolls-Royce and (a semi-privatisation) TSB. All these attracted heavy public demand, even those (like BA and Rolls) which were not heavily advertised. British Gas, which was, pulled in four and a half million shareholders – four million of whom still retained their shares three months later. One of the big surprises of the privatisation campaign, in fact, has been the willingness of the public to regard their share allocations as long-term investments. Millions of people, clearly, now have 'mini' portfolios of shares in once-nationalised industries.

But are they venturing any further afield? Until recently, the answer from most City commentators (many of whom retain an unshakeable scepticism concerning the private investor) would have been 'no'. Nonetheless, the evidence is incontrovertible. Many City firms have severely curtailed their 'no frills' dealing services (one has even pulled out), simply because the demand has proved overwhelming. Most provincial stockbrokers dealing with private clients have similarly found their antiquated administrative systems creaking under the pressure. At the same time, there has been a rush to provide beginners on the stock market with the guidance they need. Only three years ago, the novice DIY investor had very limited access to suitable

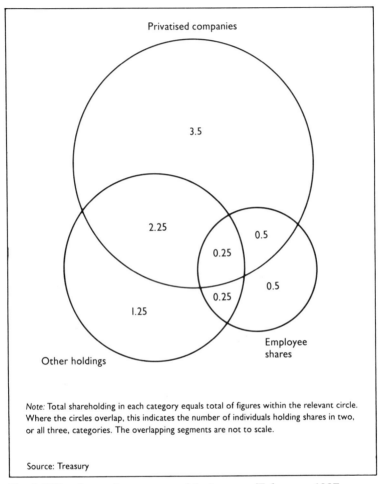

Privatised companies

3.5

2.25

0.5

0.25

0.5

0.25

1.25

Employee
shares

Other holdings

Note: Total shareholding in each category equals total of figures within the relevant circle. Where the circles overlap, this indicates the number of individuals holding shares in two, or all three, categories. The overlapping segments are not to scale.

Source: Treasury

*Fig. 1*  UK private share ownership January/February 1987.

advice. Now he will find many articles tailored to his needs in the press, and an ever-increasing number of books on the stock market available in the shops. These have obviously been produced to exploit an increasing demand for information, and are presumably not read simply out of academic interest. Undoubtedly, the general level of public interest in, and know-ledge of, the stock market and share investment has increased hugely in recent years.

There is, in fact, hard statistical evidence for the trend. A major survey sponsored by the Treasury and The Stock

Exchange in the first two months of 1987 showed that nearly 20% of the adult population (eight and a half million people aged 16 or over) now own shares – roughly treble the number in 1979. Figure 1 shows that, of these, six and a half million own shares in the privatisation issues – but only three and a half million do so exclusively. Allowing for one and a half million employee shareholders, and some overlap between the various categories, the survey showed that around four million people in Britain now own shares they have bought through the stock market. In other words, the number of 'genuine' new equity investors since 1979 appears to be one million. The vast bulk of these, in all probability, have only taken the plunge since 1985.

The survey had some interesting additional findings. Share ownership among manual workers (the marketing man's C2s, Ds and Es) has increased fastest of all – more than quintupling since 1979 to 11%. At the same time, one in ten young people aged between 16 and 24 now own shares, as do one in eight Yorkshiremen. Unsurprisingly, the figures are much higher for the professional and managerial classes, the middle-aged and those resident in the prosperous south east. Even so, if the picture is not yet one of 'people's capitalism', it's clear enough that the old image of the shareholder as a pin-striped figure toting an outsize cigar is well and truly obsolete.

## WHY OWN SHARES?

But why should anyone own shares? The answer, as almost all of the new equity investors have found out, is that it can be extremely profitable – much more profitable than most alternative forms of investment. True, most of the privatisation issues were launched at artificially cheap prices – and the market as a whole has been rising unusually fast in recent years. A repetition of this success, at least on the same scale, would seem to be unlikely – and markets can and do fall backwards. Nonetheless, the long-term trend is undeniable, as Fig. 2 shows. Since 1970, despite several ups and downs, £1,000 invested in shares would have risen, on average, to well over £10,000 by the end of 1986. The same amount, left to accumulate interest in a building society, would be worth slightly over £3,000. Admittedly, the comparison would look a lot less flattering if the cut-off point were taken in 1979 – at the end of one of the stock market's most

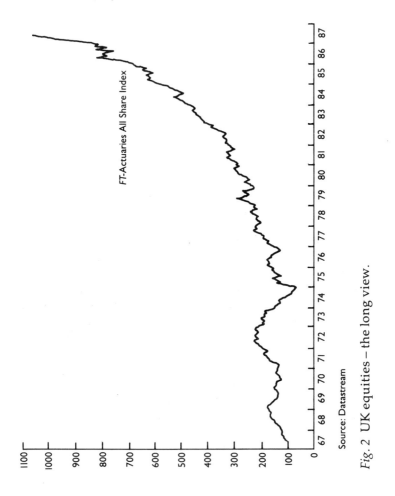

*Fig. 2* UK equities – the long view.

difficult decades. Nonetheless, the essential point remains the same. So long as the economy, and with it company profit-ability, continues to grow, the investment superiority of shares will always assert itself in the end. If the economy were to stop growing, and if profits slumped into permanent decline, there's no doubt that stock market investment would prove extremely unrewarding. But then, so would just about everything else.

The truth is that when you invest directly on the stock market, you are cutting out the middleman. When you lend money, or pay insurance premiums, or contribute to a pension fund, you do so in the expectation of a financial return. Yet that return, obviously, cannot just materialise out of thin air. The financial institutions have to work at making your investment grow – which they can only do by lending it out again at higher rates of interest (building societies and banks for example), or by investing it in property or on the stock market. Ultimately, though, the money must be earned by business. Companies are not just in business to make their managers rich. They need to make profits in order that they can pay their employees (who will have mortgage and other liabilities of their own) and also to service their loans from the banks. Over and above that, they must try to find a surplus for re-investment, and for paying some sort of return to their share-holders. As we shall see in Chapter 6, share-holders are only rarely the same people who put up the capital to start the business in the first place. That is immaterial – it is only because shares are (or one day will be) freely transferable, that investors will ever be prepared to stump up original capital. Successors or no, the share-holders own the business, take the risks, and reap the rewards. Though they are last in the queue after employees and creditors, they are entitled to any surplus. If the company goes bust, they will lose everything. But if it thrives and grows larger, they should benefit more than anyone else.

Immoral? In the first place, it is worth remembering that no one takes financial risks without the expectation of reward. If no risks are taken, enterprise becomes impossible. Secondly, it is only because companies can pass their success on to their share-holders that the insurance companies and pension funds which dominate the stock market, can offer the benefits they do. In one way or another, therefore, virtually everyone in Britain already has a vital interest in the stock market. Without the profits made on shares, pension benefits and the proceeds on insurance policies would be very much smaller.

Pensioners and policy-holders, though, are unlikely to see the full benefit of these stock market gains. After all, both pension funds and insurance companies always have heavy liabilities stretching out into the distant future, and must therefore maintain substantial 'reserves' to make sure they can meet them. In addition, they have to pay their large bureaucracies and (in many cases) the heavy costs associated with drumming up new business. Above all, there is a huge element of cross-subsidy. Policy-holders who die young, for example, receive (or at least their dependents receive) benefits out of all

proportion to their contribution to the insurance fund. Naturally, this is effectively paid for by other policy-holders. In the
same way, pensioners who die soon after retirement subsidise
those who go on for ever. In neither case can there be a direct
link between the profits earned on an investor's contributions,
and the payout he eventually receives.

Invest directly on the stock market, and you avoid most of
these complications. Naturally, you lose in terms of guarantees
– no one will promise to look after your dependents if you die,
or pay you a proportion of your salary when you retire. On the
other hand, you won't have to pay for this security. Provided
you do averagely well on the stock market, you should eventually end up better off – particularly now that PEPs offer
individuals the same tax exemptions available to the investment institutions. No one is saying that you should ignore the
need for insurance or a pension. The point is that, regarded
purely from an investment point of view, there is no longer any
reason to 'over-fund' these forms of saving beyond the bounds
of common prudence.

But surely the stock market is risky? In the short term, the
answer is 'yes' – markets move in cycles, and their relapses can
sometimes be quite severe. In the long term, though, there is no
reason to assume that the stock market is any more dangerous
than any alternative home for your savings – indeed it is
considerably less so than some. Virtually any form of investment is ultimately based on that elusive quality, 'confidence'.
Neither the banks nor the building societies can pay out what
they owe at any given time to their account-holders, for most of
their funds are lent out long term. The only way the building
societies, for example, could meet their liabilities would be to
repossess houses on a grand scale – yet even this would fail as it
would inevitably cause house prices to crash. Putting aside
such a nightmarish scenario, it's worth remembering that at
times of high inflation, building society investors have seen
their capital dwindle in real terms – while many insurance
policy-holders and pensioners have seen the value of their
'guaranteed' benefits very much reduced. Any investment
based on money is always acutely vulnerable to inflation. It's
worth remembering that an entire generation of prudent Ger-
man burghers saw their life savings annihilated in a matter of
months when the mark collapsed in 1923.

One inflation-beating alternative to money is assets – for

these should at least hold their real value. The trouble with assets, however, is that they are only worth what others are prepared to pay – and therefore also depend on confidence. The property crash of 1974 showed just how drastically (and at the time unexpectedly) even property prices can fall once this essential commodity evaporates. Housing, of course, is no exception – for the price rises of recent years have been based wholly on demand exceeding supply, and the expectation that this imbalance will continue. Where this has not applied (Aberdeen is a good recent example), houses have not only fallen in price, but in some cases have proved totally unsaleable. Houses have at least some real utility. Oddly enough, the asset which most people turn to in times of maximum uncertainty is the most useless of the lot – gold. According to some economic historians, the value of gold has more or less held steady in real terms (the odd decade or century excepted) since antiquity. In defiance of all reason, generation after generation has continued to believe in it.

Where do shares fit into this picture? In the short term, shares are vulnerable to the same sort of pressures – inflation can erode the value of dividends, and share prices are more susceptible than most to a fall-off in demand. Like any other asset, a share is only worth what someone else is willing to pay for it. Yet shares are not just passive assets like gold or bricks and mortar. They do, after all, represent ownership of a real business – a business which should continue to earn profits, and to keep paying dividends in all but the bleakest economic conditions. Provided the economy is growing (and when it isn't, few investments will be successful), those profits and dividends should at least increase in pace with inflation. Naturally, there are exceptions – companies which decline, and a few which go under. Taken in the round, however, shares will do well so long as the economy prospers. When you buy a share, you are not just acquiring a piece of paper. You are buying a slice of something real. And you are investing right at the cutting edge of economic growth.

# 2. How PEPs work

## THE BASICS

From 1 January 1987, anyone over the age of 18, resident in the UK for tax purposes, has been entitled to open a Personal Equity Plan. The plan must be operated by a manager accredited by the Inland Revenue, and is restricted to a maximum investment of £2,400 a year, or £200 per month. As originally proposed, all investments made through a plan were to be confined to ordinary shares quoted on the London Stock Exchange. This still remains the intention of the scheme, though the rules were eased slightly during the run-up to its introduction. Under current regulations, PEP investors can keep a small proportion of their holdings in cash, and another, somewhat larger proportion, in the form of unit and/or investment trusts.

All qualifying investments made through a PEP are completely exempt from both income tax on dividends (provided these are re-invested), and capital gains tax on disposals. In the former case, plan managers are required to reclaim tax already paid on dividends from the Inland Revenue.

To qualify for these tax exemptions, a PEP has to be in operation for a complete calendar year. In practice, your PEP will start accumulating tax-free from the moment the money is invested, but any reliefs will be invalidated if you withdraw funds from the plan before it has qualified. What this means, in effect, is that a PEP taken out in 1987 will not qualify until 1 January 1989 – and that if you withdraw so much as a penny before then, you will render the entire plan void. This doesn't commit the plan-holder to an entirely static investment policy, however. Provided the plan itself remains intact, the investments within it can be switched at any time. In addition, you can change your plan manager – though he is entitled to charge you for this if your plan has not yet qualified. It should be noted, too, that your alternative manager is under no compulsion to take you on his books.

The really important point to grasp is that a new plan, up to the £2,400 limit, can be opened each year. Some comment on the scheme has tended to imply that PEPs are limited to a one-off investment of £2,400 – a sum too small to attract any meaningful tax concessions. In fact, if the annual limit is considered analogous to an annual insurance premium or pension contribution, it is really quite generous – and especially so if a husband and wife (who are treated separately) both open plans and use up their full entitlement.

Once a plan has gone through its first two stages (the 'current' year, or year of investment, and the 'holding' year in which it qualifies) it becomes 'mature'. Proceeds are then eligible for withdrawal without penalty, though they can also be left to accumulate – still free of tax – for as long as the plan-holder so wishes. As each plan qualifies, so it can be merged with other mature plans into a single 'mature portfolio', where the original boundary lines between plans are no longer relevant. Figure 3 makes this more readily apparent. Each PEP can be regarded as

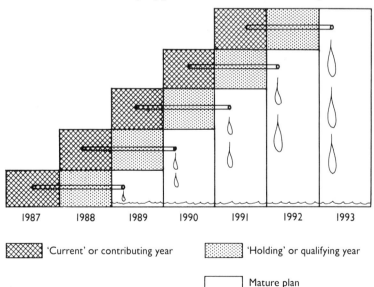

| 1987 | 1988 | 1989 | 1990 | 1991 | 1992 | 1993 |

▨▨▨ 'Current' or contributing year     ▨▨▨ 'Holding' or qualifying year

☐ Mature plan

*Fig. 3* How PEPs work.

an individual pipeline feeding funds into a unified investment pool. That pool can then be tampered with at will. Individual share-holdings can be switched, or merged – and the investor can withdraw whatever funds he likes without affecting the tax exemption of the remainder.

# THE TAX BREAKS

Even those who pay no tax may find PEPs useful, for they remove much of the administrative burden associated with share ownership. For the vast majority of people, though, the main motivation will be the tax concessions. To judge how important these are, it is necessary to know exactly what you are being protected from.

## Income tax

All investment income is taxed at the investor's top rate – for obviously it represents an addition to existing earned income. In some cases, too, this *unearned* income may be sufficient to carry an investor into a higher tax band. In the normal course of events, dividends on shares (see page 50) are paid net of tax at the basic rate, and are accompanied by a tax credit certificate stating the sum deducted. Non-taxpayers can use this tax credit to reclaim the deduction from the Inland Revenue. Higher-rate tax payers, naturally, will be liable to pay an additional sum.

Though income tax rates have come down substantially in recent years, and are expected to fall further, they remain galling enough. Higher-rate taxpayers, in particular, often pay little or no attention to yields on the grounds that most of the benefit will go straight to the Government. As a result, invest-ment decisions are seldom based on 'total return', but purely on the prospects for capital gain.

For these, PEPs clearly offer new-found freedom – as a 5% gross yield (normally worth just 2% to a 60% taxpayer) is now available in full. Looked at another way, you would have to find non-exempt investments returning 12.5% gross to produce the same effect – virtually impossible in current market conditions, and never easy to achieve without incurring considerable risk or (at the very least) forgoing any reasonable hope of capital gain. For most higher-rate taxpayers, investing via a PEP

Marginal tax rate

|  |  | 27% | 40% | 45% | 50% | 60% |
|---|---|---|---|---|---|---|
| Gross yield | 1% | £6.48 | £9.60 | £10.80 | £12.00 | £14.40 |
| | 2% | £12.96 | £19.20 | £21.60 | £24.00 | £28.80 |
| | 3% | £19.44 | £28.80 | £32.40 | £36.00 | £43.20 |
| | 4% | £25.92 | £38.40 | £43.20 | £48.00 | £57.60 |
| | 5% | £32.40 | £48.00 | £54.00 | £60.00 | £72.00 |
| | 6% | £38.88 | £57.60 | £64.80 | £72.00 | £86.40 |
| | 7% | £45.36 | £67.20 | £75.60 | £84.00 | £100.80 |
| | 8% | £51.84 | £76.80 | £86.40 | £96.00 | £115.20 |
| | 9% | £58.32 | £86.40 | £97.20 | £108.00 | £129.60 |
| | 10% | £64.80 | £96.00 | £108.00 | £120.00 | £144.00 |

*Fig. 4* Annual income tax saving per £2,400 PEP investment.

should add appreciably to total investment returns, and allow greater flexibility in terms of investment choice.

Most people, of course, pay income tax only at the basic rate – and with this down to 27% in 1987–88, the immediate gain becomes much less obvious. £2,400 invested at 5%, for example, will only produce a tax saving of £32.40 in the first year (see Fig. 4) – liable to be swallowed up (and more) by many plan managers' initial charges. Thereafter, the sums depend entirely on a number of variables – the rate of tax, dividend growth, the manager's annual charge, and even capital appreciation. As an illustration, it might be reasonable to assume a reduction in tax to 25%, an annual management charge of 1% of the PEP's total value, and annual dividend and capital growth of 10%. After one year, assuming initial charges were paid on top of the £2,400 invested, the annual charge is likely to be slightly over £27, and the tax saving £33. In these circumstances, the income tax saving should pull further ahead of the management charge year by year – but only if tax rates do not fall further, and dividends are not outpaced by capital growth. Capital growth, obviously, will boost any charge levied as a percentage of the PEP's value.

This saving can be boosted slightly by selecting a plan manager who charges a flat management fee rather than one worked out on a percentage basis. In addition, it is always possible to find shares yielding in excess of 5% – though even that figure is well above average in today's stock market. Nonetheless, it seems pretty clear that the overall benefit to most basic-rate payers will be small while both tax rates and dividend yields remain low – at least it will be in the early years. Looked at in a more positive light, of course, it can be argued that the income tax exemption alone will usually mop up all management fees. Effectively that means that the other benefits of PEPs – simple administration, professional fund management (if required), and, where applicable, exceptionally cheap dealing costs will be in the scheme for nothing. Above all, it leaves the field clear for the capital gains tax exemption.

## Capital gains tax

This levy on capital profits has never crippled anyone, but it remains an unmitigated pest. The capital gains tax (CGT) rate is 30% on all capital gains over a £6,700 threshold (1987–88), though the threshold is now raised annually in line with inflation (in tax year 1986–87 it was £6,300). In addition, investors are allowed to raise the purchase cost of their investments in line with the retail price index (RPI) before calculating their 'real' gain. In practice, the complications are even more fiendish – for any capital losses can be used to offset CGT, and these can be carried forward into future tax years.

It is often said that CGT is easy to avoid. What commentators really mean is that it is usually *possible* to avoid CGT – but only after much time and trouble, the expense of hiring an accountant (only the keenest of number-crunchers can face working out their own potential liability), and usually after performing contortions on the stock market. Keen to use their annual exemption to the full, many investors make a point of taking profits up to the limit in one tax year, and then buy back the shares involved (at a higher purchase price) in the next. This 'bed and breakfasting' manoeuvre keeps CGT bills low for all but the wealthiest investors, though it obviously has its costs. On each occasion, a new set of dealing charges is incurred, and the 'turn' (or difference between buying and selling prices) has to be paid. Possibly the most irritating aspect of CGT however, is the way it tends to interfere with investment decisions. Many investors find that they cannot bear to take any profits liable to CGT, and therefore fail to take advantage of good switching or selling opportunities. The result, in many cases, is that they end up losing more money to the market than they ever would have done to the taxman.

PEPs, of course, are CGT exempt and any investments made through them avoid all such complications. For anyone actually paying CGT, taking out a PEP should be virtually compulsory – for the Revenue is simply inviting you to 'shelter' £2,400 per year. To achieve the maximum benefit from this in relation to an existing portfolio, it may pay to use a PEP as the second leg of a bed and breakfasting exercise. Any share which has risen strongly, and still looks promising, can be sold in the market to use up the annual CGT limit, then repurchased tax-exempt through a PEP. This has the additional advantage of flexibility, for there is no longer any need to make the initial sale close to the end of the tax year.

Everyone admits that PEPs are a free gift for those already paying CGT. A big majority of investors, however, do not pay the tax – and for them, PEPs are often dismissed as an irrelevance. Nonetheless, it's worth asking *why* so few are caught in the tax net. Apart from those performing gymnastics on the stock market, many people undoubtedly take on other investment commitments for the sake of their tax efficiency. Pensions are perhaps a special case. But most insurance or insurance-linked policies – when used purely as savings vehicles – are probably taken out because the proceeds are tax free. In addition, some people undoubtedly buy a more expensive house than they need – again, because when they eventually 'trade down', they know that the surplus profit will be exempt from CGT. For anyone in these categories, PEPs have made direct stock market investment a competitive alternative. At the very least, it need no longer be rejected on tax grounds alone.

Even the automatic assumption that the man in the street will never be liable to CGT may be misplaced. In the late 1980s, after all, we have reached a time when the first generation of owner-occupiers is beginning to die off, making the inheritance of large estates much more common than hitherto. In many cases, heirs have already bought their own houses, and will therefore wish to convert their parents' property into cash for investment elsewhere. In London and the south east, especially, inheritances of £50,000 to £100,000 are no longer unusual – certainly they do not begin to imply exceptional family wealth. It's worth remembering that £50,000 invested in shares need only rise by 13.5% before a CGT liability arises. In recent years, a gain of that order would have been achieved very quickly – though there is obviously no guarantee that the market will be so strong in future.

PEPs, then, are definitely worth considering by anyone who suspects that he might have a CGT problem in the future. Obviously, you cannot invest a large inherited sum until it materialises. What you can do, in the meantime, is shelter as much of your existing savings as possible – for when the capital injection finally arrives, it will render the whole of your investments liable to CGT. Anyone in this boat who already invests on the stock market, or who intends to, may later regret not using up his annual PEP entitlement to the fullest possible extent.

Finally, what about those who can only accumulate capital out of income? For the vast majority of people in the real world, the annual PEP limit of £2,400 (often derided in the City as ludicrously small) will seem generous enough – particularly so, when it's considered that a husband and wife team can contribute £4,800. In only ten years, therefore, the PEP scheme allows a couple to salt away a net investment of £48,000. Applying standard (if not terribly meaningful) growth assumptions of 10% a year in both capital and dividends, that should produce a tax exempt fund of something like £100,000. If the stock market continues to perform as it did in the early 1980s, of course, the figure would be very much higher. Nonetheless, even that £100,000 would be liable to a very heavy CGT bill if it were withdrawn at once. Assuming a stable inflation rate of 5%, and no change in the threshold indexation policy, CGT will cut in on annual gains over £10,900 in ten years' time.

One crucial aspect of tax, often overlooked in the midst of number-crunching, is the hassle factor. CGT, of course, is notoriously complicated – worse even than VAT according to some people. Yet even income tax on dividends requires full details of receipts to be entered on an investor's annual tax return, and the retention of tax credits for reference. One of the beauties of investing through a PEP is that you need have no contact whatsoever with the Inland Revenue. For some people, especially those requiring an accountant to sort out their investment tax liabilities, this alone may justify a plan manager's fees.

## THE DETAILS

As originally conceived, the PEP scheme was no doubt intended to be entirely straightforward – investors could invest up to £2,400 a year on the stock market, and their profits would be tax-free. *Finis.* Unfortunately, the small print demonstrates Whitehall at its worst. During the consultation phase which followed the scheme's announcement, many potential managers raised the practical difficulties involved. Even the maximum contribution of £2,400 was considered far too low to provide a reasonable spread of investments, and would confine many very small investors to a single share. In addition, there had to be rules about cash holdings. In practical terms, small monthly contributions could not be invested until they'd had time to build up. Nor was it reasonable to expect investors selling shares within a PEP to find immediate replacements. Though answers to these and many other problems were found, the end result suggests elaborate compromises in the committee room.

Most of the complexities contained in the small print of the PEP regulations are of concern only to plan managers. Here, it is only necessary to comment on some of the major rules which may affect a plan-holder's investment decisions.

## Investment limits

Though there is no minimum limit, in practice no fund manager will accept a contribution of less than £20 per month or £200 in an annual lump sum. These, of course, are absolute minimums – most managers require larger commitments, and a few will only take on clients willing to invest the maximum £2,400 in a lump sum. The upper limit itself only relates to money intended for investment. In order to maximise the tax concessions, many plan managers will allow investors to pay their initial charges on top.

## Cash holdings

This was one of the main areas of dispute between the Revenue and potential fund managers, and the end result is nothing if not complicated.

Under the regulations, all money paid into a PEP up to the £2,400 limit can now be held in the form of cash throughout the 'current' or contributing year. Once the limit has been reached, however, the PEP must be invested within a calendar month in qualifying securities. This concession is undoubtedly of great benefit to high income tax payers, for interest rates available in the cash market are much higher than those currently prevailing in shares, capital is secure, and all proceeds still qualify for tax relief. A rate of 8% on cash held within a PEP equates to 11% gross for basic-rate taxpayers, and a mighty 20% for those on a marginal tax rate of 60%.

One important point to note about this loophole is that it only lasts so long as none of your PEP funds are invested on the stock market (and in any case not beyond the year in which you contribute). Thereafter, funds held *permanently* in cash cannot exceed 10% of the value of your PEP portfolio. This is assessed according to its valuation at the previous 31 December – and will not alter throughout the year. If, for example, a PEP is worth £3,000 at the end of its current year, the maximum cash permitted will be £300 throughout the following 'holding' year. If it rises to £4,000 by the end of the holding year, the limit will abruptly jump from £300 to £400 on 1 January of year three. Just to confuse matters further, the limit will be reduced immediately to take account of any withdrawals you make. Take £1,000 out of that £4,000 PEP soon after it has matured, and your cash limit drops straight back to £300. It must be emphasised that these limits do not apply to cash raised temporarily from share sales. Provided funds are re-invested within 28 days, they can be parked meanwhile in an interest-bearing cash account. In theory, there is nothing to stop you putting your entire PEP into cash for a month. Plan managers are obliged to hold any long-term cash in your plan in a specially-designated sterling deposit account which pays interest gross.

## Unit and investment trusts

One of the main criticisms of the PEP scheme, as originally proposed, was that it explicitly forbade investment in any form of pooled investment fund. PEP investors were to be clearly identified as the beneficial owners of all shares held to their account. Though this attitude was entirely reasonable in theory (after all, the scheme was designed to encourage direct equity investment), City fund managers successfully argued that it would force smaller investors into speculating on a single share. Accordingly, yet another awkward compromise was reached.

Under present regulations, £420 or 25% of the value of a PEP (whichever is greater), can be invested in unit or investment trusts. Up to an investment of £1,680, therefore, the limit is £420 – above that, and it gradually rises to £600.

Unit and investment trusts are both managed funds which invest in a wide spread of equities, though there are important differences between them. A unit trust is an 'open-ended' fund of fluctuating size. Units are created to reflect any incoming investment, and cancelled as unit-holders withdraw. The price of a unit is determined simply by dividing the value of the trust's portfolio by the number of units in issue – though there is a 'spread' of around 6 to 7% between the 'offer' (or buying) price and the 'bid' (or selling) price. This difference represents the fund manager's initial charges, dealing costs, and the price spread on the shares in the fund's portfolio. In addition, there is a small annual charge (usually 1.5%), deducted from dividends.

Investment trusts, in contrast, are 'closed-end' funds. Essentially, they are investment companies which restrict their activities to investing in shares. Like any other company, they raise capital from the public and their shares are then quoted on The

Stock Exchange. The price of the shares depends ultimately on the value of the Trust's portfolio – divided by the number of shares in issue, this will give a 'net asset value' (or NAV) per share. In practice, of course, the price of a trust's share – like any other – is governed solely by supply and demand. As a rule, investment trusts tend to stand at a discount to their assets of between 15 and 25% – which means, in effect, that their share-holders are buying into an equity portfolio on the cheap. For this reason, investment trust yields tend to be somewhat higher than the market average (you may have £100 worth of shares working for you at a cost of only £80), though fluctuations in the discount mean that you are not guaranteed to see the full rise in the value of the underlying portfolio. There are no initial management charges to pay, and the annual charge – again deducted from dividends – is usually very low indeed.

On the whole (though it is a gross generalisation), investment trusts tend to be larger than unit trusts, and spread their investment nets more widely. A typical example might have 50% of its funds invested in the UK, another 25% in the US, and the remainder split between the Far East and Europe. Apart from 'international' funds, most unit trusts are more specialised. They range from 'general' funds, aiming at a very wide spread of UK equities, to go-getting performance funds, to funds specialising in particular foreign markets like Japan, the US or Australia. There are even funds which only invest in certain sectors of the world economy – high technology, say, or natural resources.

Small investors in PEPs are probably best advised to put a high proportion of their funds into either unit or investment trusts, as this will guarantee them a wide (and therefore relatively safe) spread of investments. Other investors, though, should also find the concession useful. Oddly enough, the rules do not restrict investment to trusts wholly (or even partially) invested in UK shares – and this exemption can clearly be useful for channelling funds abroad if conditions at home look bleak. Equally, some unit trusts specialise in gilts, convertibles and other forms of high-income investments, allowing PEP holders to boost the overall yield of their plans. What the taxman giveth, however, the taxman also taketh away. One quirk in the rules is that funds invested in equities cannot later be switched into unit or investment trusts. There is no restriction on switching in the other direction, however, or on switching between trusts.

## Equities

Apart from the allowances above, all other funds contributed to a PEP must be invested in the ordinary shares of UK quoted companies. These must either be listed on The Stock Exchange, or else traded on the Unlisted Securities Market (USM). The difference between these two categories is largely semantic. Though USM companies are generally smaller and younger than their 'fully' listed colleagues, shares in both types of company are dealt in on the stock market in exactly the same way.

Excluded by the rules are many other types of security quoted on The Stock Exchange. Gilts are out, as are other fixed-interest stocks, preference shares (which pay out a fixed dividend), convertibles (fixed-interest securities convertible into ordinary shares), and speculative esoterica like options and warrants. So, of course, are all foreign shares. Though many multinationals now have a listing on the London Stock Exchange, only those incorporated in the UK qualify for PEP investment.

## Switching

The regulations specifically forbid investors to switch existing equity holdings directly into a PEP. All contributions must be in the form of cash – meaning, in effect, that you will have to sell shares on the market, put the proceeds in a PEP, then re-purchase through the plan. Once a PEP is in place, there are no restrictions on how often you can switch between equity investments. The only rule is that you cannot hold cash for more than a month, so any proceeds from sales have to be re-invested fairly promptly.

## Frequency of investment

The rules themselves do not dictate how often a PEP investor can contribute to a current plan, though plan managers clearly have their own restrictions in order to keep administrative costs down. Most offer a choice between monthly contributions or an annual lump-sum payment, though many of the smaller schemes are lump-sum only. A few managers offer quarterly or half-yearly payments.

# 3. PEP investors

## PUTTING PEPS TO USE

No one can get the best out of any investment unless he has some idea of the result he is trying to achieve. As a hangover, perhaps, from the traumatic 1970s, the magic words 'tax break' still ring very sweetly in British ears. Yet tax concessions on their own are seldom enough. If they lead to bad or inappropriate investment decisions, they can positively damage their recipients' financial well being.

As was made clear in the previous chapter, the only people who can be certain to benefit immediately from PEPs are those already liable for capital gains tax. Equally, it can be safely asserted that anyone with only £500 to spare and likely to withdraw it within a year, would be extremely ill-advised to take out a plan. Most people, though, will fall somewhere in the middle. There are really two key points to remember. The first is that the tax concessions are only available after at least one complete calendar year, and will be revoked if a plan is violated before its maturity. Given managers' initial charges, and the fact that many of them invoke an 'early withdrawal' charge, it's clear that a PEP is a thoroughly unsuitable home for any cash which may be needed in a hurry. Secondly, the full impact of the Revenue's largesse will only be felt after several years have passed. Eventually, if the stock market continues to do well, the tax savings should be very substantial indeed. Those who invest a sizeable sum in a new PEP each year, and keep doing so over the long haul, are unlikely to regret their choice of savings vehicle.

A comparison between PEPs and other long-term investment schemes shows that they do have certain advantages over the main alternatives. For sheer tax-avoiding power, it is obvious they cannot compete with pension schemes – for these, within generous limits, allow the investor to write off the whole of his annual contribution against his highest rate of income tax. Yet pension schemes do have significant drawbacks – not least of which is that they must ultimately be used to fund a pension. The return is thus an entirely unknown quantity. Though the pensioner is entitled to a substantial cash lump sum on retirement, the bulk of his accumulated funds must be used to provide an annuity. Should he and his spouse die shortly after retirement, most of the benefits from years of saving will be lost – not just to the pensioner (who isn't in a position to worry), but also to his heirs. It's worth remembering, too, that pensions seldom become a pressing concern until later in life. Younger people usually have more immediate financial concerns – getting housed, getting their children educated and so forth – and in any case find it difficult to accord much importance to a retirement which still seems very remote. To be sure, the pensions industry has worked hard to give its products youth appeal – concocting 'loan-back' facilities and pension mortgages. The problem is that such uses of pension plans are vulnerable politically – even from a Conservative government. A growing number of people in high places regard them as misuses of the very generous tax concessions on offer.

The nearest equivalent to PEPs are probably life assurance policies – at least those endowment or unit-linked plans intended mainly for use as savings vehicles. Though these lost a major selling point with the abolition of LAPR (life assurance premium relief) in the 1984 Budget, they are still in a position to pay out to policy-holders tax-free. Nonetheless, it is possible to regard PEPs as in many ways superior. In the first place, life assurance policies do have to incorporate a measure of insurance, however small, in order to qualify for their reliefs. In many cases, this is irrelevant to their real purpose and unwanted by the policy-holder – yet it still has to be paid for. Secondly, policies are expensive to set up and, in many cases, are intensively marketed. These costs are usually passed on immediately to the policy-holder in the form of a heavy 'front-end load' charging structure – often eating up his first three monthly premiums entirely. Thirdly, many policies – especially the traditional endowment variety – are pretty inflexible. Withdrawals from the policy early in its life are likely to show a very meagre return, and much of the eventual profit is paid in the form of 'terminal' bonuses. To qualify for those, you have to be sure of sticking with the policy right to the end of its life. In a rapidly changing world, such absolute certainty about the next 10, 15 or 20 years is given to few.

On all these counts, PEPs can compete effectively. All sums saved through a plan will be properly invested, and not used to serve some ancillary purpose. The 'front-end' load (represented by the plan managers' initial fees) varies from plan to plan – but in some cases is astonishingly low. Above all, PEPs are much more flexible. A great deal of the criticism of the scheme has focused on its restrictions during the first two (the current and holding) years of an individual plan's life. Much less has been said about the freedom offered the investor once his plan has matured and been merged with others in an integrated portfolio. Though he should normally be aiming to hold his investment for the long term, he will lose nothing if his circumstances suddenly change and he finds it necessary to withdraw funds. He can even change his plan manager if dissatisfied with his performance, or if he finds a better-looking deal elsewhere.

Because PEPs are still so new, there has been little discussion about the uses they might serve. In time, this is certain to change. At present, much of the financial services industry regards the PEP scheme as an unmitigated burden – the administration costs of managing a host of small equity-based accounts mean that very few plan managers are currently making a profit. After a few years, when some plans will have reached sizeable proportions, this attitude is bound to change – mature portfolios worth £25,000, say, will be regarded as a prize catch by some firms. When this point is reached (or, more probably, sometime beforehand), the customary ingenuity of the financial services industry can be expected to come into play. The City marketing men who brought you unit-linked insurance and pension mortgages are certainly not going to leave PEPs alone – already there is talk of loan-back facilities.

In the meantime, would-be PEP investors should consider their own uses for the scheme – more constructive uses, perhaps, than a vague aspiration to save tax. Two immediately spring to mind – coping with mid-life expenses and supplementing pensions.

## Mid-life expenses

Most people, once they have got themselves decently housed and have started to raise a family, don't immediately start planning for retirement. If they have some money to spare, their next aspirations will probably lie rather closer to hand – a private secondary education for their children, for example, or a weekend home in the country. In many cases, these ambitions are only going to be fulfilled after several years' hard savings.

The traditional reply to the big mid-life expense has been the ten-to-fifteen-year insurance policy. However elaborate or specifically-directed (a school-fees plan, for example, is basically an endowment policy with frills) this will still have the drawbacks described above – though it must be said that some people welcome the discipline an insurance policy imposes. Others, desiring more flexibility, save through unit trusts or invest directly on the stock market – though the tax advantages in the former case are small, and in the latter case nil. It shouldn't be forgotten that although a unit trust pays no capital gains tax on its share dealings, a unit-holder is liable for his own gains on the units when he withdraws his funds. Only the ultra-cautious will always accumulate their savings through the building society. This is neither tax efficient, nor – in the long term – competitive on investment grounds.

In many ways, PEPs seem to offer an ideal compromise between these approaches to medium/long-term investment. Over time, the tax advantages will become much more readily apparent – and the desire to preserve them may at least provide an element of discipline for those in need of it. Should plans change, however, or an emergency arise, the PEP investor still has a large element of flexibility – if he withdraws, all he will lose, in most cases, is the opportunity to accumulate more tax-free benefits. Meanwhile, he has considerable choice over the way he wishes his funds to be invested. He can either back his own judgement on the stock market, or else secure professional fund management at a very low cost.

## Supplementing pensions

Given the size of the maximum PEP limit, there's no doubt that a series of plans – if started early enough – could alone support anybody's retirement needs. After 30 years, after all, a PEP investor can contribute a maximum of £72,000 – a sum almost certain to have grown into several hundreds of thousands of pounds after three decades' tax-free accumulation. Nonetheless, this would not be a particularly sensible use of the various tax concessions on offer – as we have seen, PEPs cannot compete with pension schemes when it comes to saving specifically for retirement. That said, they may still have a useful supplementary role to play.

The marketing of pensions, especially to high-rate taxpayers, naturally concentrates on the excellent tax shelter provided for income while they are still earning. Less publicised is the fact that the pension benefits themselves are taxable – at least, the major annuity element is. As a result, it is quite feasible to over-fund a pension plan – saving tax at a high marginal rate in the run-up to retirement, only to lose much of it afterwards as the pension is paid out. Admittedly, this is only a problem for the wealthy – relatively few people continue to pay high rates of tax after they've stopped earning. Nonetheless, there are problems with pensions which affect everyone. If you die early, you (or rather your estate) may lose benefits you saved for long and hard. If you die late, you may see the real value of your pension severely eroded. Even with an annual inflation rate of 5%, it will only take 15 years to reduce an income of £15,000 to slightly less than £7,000 in real terms. Though there are partial solutions to this problem (some annuities, starting at a lower level, allow for a small annual increase), none of them could cope with a sustained resurgence of double-digit inflation.

Once again, PEPs should be able to play an important role – even if only a supporting one. Under the current rules, it is not possible to withdraw tax-free dividends immediately from a plan (even a mature one) – but there is nothing to stop the investor making capital withdrawals. By building up a sizeable PEP portfolio, and then switching into relatively high-yielding investments on retirement, the investor should be able to produce an efficient income-producing fund which is virtually self-replenishing. A fund worth £50,000, for example, invested in shares yielding 7%, would produce an annual income of £3,500 (equivalent to £4,800 at the basic rate of tax). That figure could be expected to grow in future years (albeit at a slower rate than on lower-yielding shares) – as would the capital value of the fund. By withdrawing an equivalent sum in capital, the investor would not affect his tax concessions, nor would he damage the overall value of his fund. Indeed, if history is any guide, he might easily get away with withdrawals of 10% annually.

To accumulate a fund worth £50,000, on fairly conservative growth assumptions, should not take an investor much longer than ten years if he invests up to his annual PEP limit. Using his spouse's entitlement as well, of course, he could double the sum over the same period. For those who have already funded a reasonable pension in the normal way, also establishing a decent-sized PEP in the final years to retirement must make sense. Not only will all withdrawals be free of tax, but the capital will still be available for transmission to heirs. In due course, it is certain that many plan managers will follow their unit trust colleagues, and organise formal 'regular withdrawal' schemes for mature PEP portfolios.

## BESPOKE PLANS – OR OFF THE PEG?

Though shares held through a PEP are registered in the name of the plan manager, the PEP investor is still the 'beneficial' owner with an identifiable individual interest. This differs from investment in a unit trust, say, where the unit-holder's interest in the trust's shares is indirect.

Nonetheless, many PEPs have been organised in such a way that they are effectively fund management vehicles. Invest through one of these 'discretionary' plans, and all decisions about which shares to invest in, and when to switch them, are left to the plan manager. The alternative, 'non-discretionary', plans allow investors to make their own choices – though these will normally have to be from a list of large companies selected by the manager. Which to choose – bespoke, or off the peg?

The answer really depends on what interest you have in the stock market, and how knowledgeable you are. If stocks and shares bore you rigid, or you simply don't have the time to spare, there is no point whatsoever in trying to do your own thing.

But what if you *are* interested in the stock market, yet know little about it? As the second half of this book is intended to show, no one has to be a genius to understand how the market and shares work – or how to invest successfully. Nonetheless, there's no doubt that a little experience counts for any amount of theory. Beginners in equity investment, having read up on their subject, are often over-confident of success – yet quickly make silly mistakes they would certainly avoid a year later. The stock market is really more about psychology than economics, and it takes time to gain a 'feel' for its moods.

Mistakes can be costly, but they can also be educational: most successful investors learned their craft the hard way. If you are keen to gain experience immediately, most non-discretionary plans will ease you into the stock market at the shallow end. They will restrict your choice to relatively-safe 'blue chip' companies, and many of them will provide newsletters to help guide your decisions. If this still goes beyond your current level of confidence, then invest in a discretionary scheme – but watch what your manager does, and try to learn from the reasons he gives for his investment decisions. Before too long, if you follow your plan with interest, you will probably start thinking you could do a better job. You might well be wrong, but at that point you are ready to strike out on your own. Some PEP managers run both discretionary and non-discretionary plans, and will allow you to switch between the two. Even if not, you are always entitled to go elsewhere – and there's no reason why your second plan should be of the same type as your first. If you do open a discretionary plan, make sure it is a genuine one offering a decent spread of shares. Investors with no other exposure to the stock market should certainly avoid any plan containing only two or three shares. These are designed primarily for the plan manager's convenience, not the novice's security.

The man who already invests on his own behalf in the stock market is in an entirely different category. If, like many private investors, he enjoys the thrills and spills of investing in small companies, he will have to join one of the very few schemes (as yet) which will give him unlimited freedom of action. Alternatively, if he always keeps part of his portfolio in blue chips, it might make more sense to go for one of the bigger, though more restricted, schemes where he can enjoy very low dealing costs. Even discretionary plans may have a role to play. Many investors hand over a large proportion of their investment funds to professional managers (via unit or investment trusts) for the sake of security, regarding the remainder as 'fun money' with which to play the market. There is no reason why this managed element should not be transferred to a discretionary PEP plan, where it will enjoy superior tax benefits, and (in many cases) lower management charges.

# 4. PEP managers

## APPROVED OPERATORS

Obviously, not just anyone can set himself up as a manager of
PEP schemes. To qualify, a plan manager must be an authorised
dealer in securities or a professional financial adviser, and must
obtain registration from the Inland Revenue before he can offer
plans to the public.

In practice, PEPs are offered by a wide range of financial
institutions – many instantly familiar to the man in the street,
some less so. In the early months of the scheme, all the main
clearing banks were involved, as were many fund management
groups, stockbrokers, insurance companies, building societies,
financial intermediaries (including insurance brokers) and
small licensed dealers. Not all institutions offering PEPs are
actually involved in the fund management, or even the administration of plans. The international fund management group,
Fidelity, for example, runs plans marketed by the Abbey
National and several stockbrokers.

According to one government official involved in establishing the scheme, no plan manager was expected to show a profit
on his PEP services within the first three years. The administrative burden is disproportionately heavy on brand-new plans,
and managers cannot recover their costs in full without
destroying the tax benefits. Accordingly, plan managers tend to
divide into two camps – the enthusiasts (who hope to use PEPs
as a worthwhile 'loss-leader', pulling in new clients and eventually becoming profitable in their own right), and those who
reluctantly provide plans because they feel they must, or fear
that they will lose clients if they don't. Unsurprisingly, this
difference is reflected in the changes levied, and in the range of
ancillary services provided. It should be noted, too, that several

schemes – especially those run by smaller stockbrokers – are exclusively in-house, available only to existing clients.

An opinion poll, taken after PEPs had been running for a month, showed that the most popular drawers of custom were the high-street clearing banks. Certainly, the banks take a favourable long-term view of the PEP scheme, seeing it as an important means of increasing their share of the personal financial services market. Accordingly, most of them have taken the trouble to produce highly competitive schemes – and have marketed them intensively.

## THE SCHEMES AVAILABLE

Virtually every PEP scheme has its individual characteristics, though they all fall into one of four categories. Essentially, the choice is between discretionary schemes, 'restricted choice' non-discretionary schemes, DIY schemes, and Unit Trust only schemes.

### Discretionary

As we have seen, discretionary schemes are those where the plan manager is left to make all the management decisions. It is doubtful that this was what the Chancellor really intended when PEPs were first mooted, but they are undoubtedly popular with plan managers – for they simplify the administration considerably. It must be said, though, that they are also highly popular with the public. An Inland Revenue survey at the end of January 1987 showed that over three-quarters of plans taken out in the first month were discretionary.

Anyone wanting a discretionary scheme should be aware that they differ widely. Among the schemes offered in the early months, the number of shares held in a plan ranged from as low as one to as high as twenty-four – most offering somewhere between three and ten. In addition, many schemes will automatically invest up to the permitted maximum in unit and/or investment trusts. PEP investors who already have exposure to the stock market will not find this somewhat limited range too galling – from their own dealings, they will know that investing less than £1,000 (or, stretching a point, £500) in any one share is rarely cost effective. In addition, of course, their other investments outside the PEP will spread the overall risk.

Investors whose PEP represents their only holding in shares are best advised to go for plans which offer the widest range (there is a reasonable choice in the eight to ten bracket) – combined, if possible, with unit and/or investment trusts. This won't help you if the whole stock market falls. But it provides you with some protection against your plan manager making a disastrous mistake. No one, not even the most experienced professional, is immune from buying the odd dud share. If he should blunder badly with one of, say, three shares held in your PEP, it will soon look a very sick investment indeed. On the other hand, risk and reward do go together – your plan has an equal chance of outperforming spectacularly.

It is important to realise that the investment skills of fund managers vary very widely. Of course, with PEPs so new, only those taking out a plan in 1988 or later will have access to meaningful 'league tables' directly comparing past performance. In addition, most of the big plan managers also run unit trusts, and here it may be possible to form a more rounded impression. Most large public libraries have the latest Unit Trust Yearbook, and maybe also a recent copy of *Money Management* magazine, both of which offer comparative performance tables stretching back years. You will not be comparing like with like (most of the bigger unit trusts have portfolios containing up to 100 shares, or more), but it should at least be possible to form an overall impression of a management group's expertise relative to others. Where unit trusts are involved within a PEP, of course, you can make direct comparisons between competing funds.

At the end of the day, it is the performance of your investments which will determine your return – and, for that matter, the size of your tax concessions. Given the choice between a top-notch fund manager in an indifferent scheme, and an uninspired fund manager in an ideal scheme, you should choose performance every time. When comparing annual charges, especially, discretionary PEP investors should remember that it is nothing for a share price to fluctuate by 1 or 2% in a *day*.

## Non-discretionary – restricted choice

In order to keep their costs down, the majority of plan managers allowing investors to make their own decisions have felt it necessary to limit their options. Given, in theory, that there are well over 3,000 eligible shares for plan-holders to choose from, this is understandable – though undoubtedly frustrating for determined individualists.

All restricted-choice schemes present plan-holders with a list of shares to choose from. The most common number is 30 (usually the constituents of the FT-30 Share Index), though it can be considerably higher. Save & Prosper, for example, recently gave its plan-holders a list of 70. Whatever the number, the choice is basically restricted to blue chip companies – large, relatively safe and (for the most part) unexciting investments.

The number of shares which can be held in a non-discretionary scheme varies from just one to a very generous twenty-four – though most fall between three and eight. It should be noted, however, that several schemes levy a small charge on any additional share-holdings over a low limit to deter plan-holders from becoming an administrative nuisance. Policy with regard to unit or investment trusts varies widely. Many large PEP managers will give their plan-holders a free run of their wide ranging in-house trusts. A few make no provision for unit trust investment at all.

The narrow-spread problem for most non-discretionary plan-holders is no different in essentials from that facing discretionary clients. The one big difference is that you, and nobody else, will be responsible for any disasters – or, for that matter, any triumphs. The choice of scheme, then, will not depend on the plan manager's investment skills – but on his cost structure, the flexibility he allows, and the desirability of his back-up services. One important point for existing equity investors to note is the dealing charge. Some PEP managers (like most stockbrokers) still charge private clients at the old minimum commission rates – 1.65% on the value of any stock market transaction up to £7,000. Several, though, offer a significant discount on this figure – on occasions falling below 1%. Investors who already switch fairly frequently between blue chips should therefore make a considerable saving on costs by taking out a suitable plan.

## Non-discretionary – DIY

Sadly, the number of PEP schemes which allow investors a completely free hand is extremely low at present. Among the very biggest schemes, the National Westminster Bank's *Share Plan* comes close – for it will at least allow you to select any share you like beyond its normal list, albeit at an additional charge of £10. On the other hand, any one PEP is limited to just two share-holdings, and there is no provision for investment in unit trusts.

Apart from a few very minor schemes (mostly run by stock-brokers exclusively for their existing clients), only a few small securities houses in the City and elsewhere offer PEP investors absolute freedom of choice.

It is almost certain that as PEP portfolios grow in size, many of the current restrictions will be lifted, for individual plans will become more economic to administer. In all probability, too, given the plan-holder's right to transfer his PEP investments, it won't be long before the more aggressive plan managers start trying to poach large 'mature' portfolios from their competitors. In these circumstances, assuming that appreciable demand for DIY schemes exists, they are bound to be provided in much greater numbers.

## Unit-trust only schemes

As we saw in Chapter 2, one of the harshest criticisms levelled at PEPs during the consultation phase was the unsuitability of direct equity investment for very small investors. The result was the unit/investment trust allowance of £420, or a quarter of a PEP's value – whichever is higher. Having got their way, unit trust managers have not been slow to exploit the loophole.

All unit trust only PEPs are necessarily limited to a maximum investment of £420. Some managers require this to be paid in as a lump sum, others will accept a monthly contribution of £35. The underlying trust will either be set up specifically for PEP purposes, or else be one of a large management group's wide range. Administration of these schemes is relatively straightforward (unit-holders are not direct beneficial owners of the trust's investments), and most plan managers have therefore made no additional PEP levy on top of their existing charge for managing the trust. Compared with most equity-based PEPs, this is quite steep – usually 5% initially, then 0.75% to 1.5% annually (deducted from the trust's dividend income). Even so, PEP investors are no worse off in this respect than other unit-holders – and clearly better off insofar as they enjoy tax exemption on both dividends and capital gains.

Admittedly, the tax benefit on such a small sum is likely to be very low in the initial years. In year one, a unit trust PEP yielding 5% (after charges) would produce a princely income tax saving of just £5.67 for a basic-rate taxpayer. This will, however, grow in line with dividends, and as new plans are added. Unit trust PEP investors, too, can invest wholly in trusts specialising in high-yielding securities, thus boosting their benefits. For most people investing only £420 a year, CGT is highly unlikely to come into the picture.

Are unit trust PEPs worth the bother? The answer would probably be no, except that there isn't any bother. If you are thinking of saving small amounts through unit trusts anyway, you might as well have the tax benefits on offer. The only real disadvantage is that your funds will be tied up until each plan matures. Naturally, these remarks only apply to those who expect to remain small savers for ever. If you can foresee a time when you might have substantial tax liabilities, the sooner you can get a PEP under way the better. In the years when you can't afford to save much, a unit trust based vehicle is probably the simplest solution.

Unit trust only schemes which 'double charge' – i.e. for managing the PEP as well as the unit trust – should generally be avoided, unless investment performance is considered truly superior.

## HOW PEPs ARE MANAGED

Before going on to look at the vexed question of charges, it's worth considering what PEP managers have to do to justify them. First and foremost, they have to administer hundreds, or even thousands, of very small, and maybe quite complex, equity portfolios – and to ensure that their plan-holders remain within the scheme's complicated rules. Obviously, this burden is easier for discretionary managers, for they can make all the investment decisions, and all their plan-holders will have the same investments. Non-discretionary managers, however – especially those offering a wider range of investment options – will have to administer a variety of individual portfolios. Though they will have bought the shares in bulk on the stock market, and had them registered in their own name, they have to ensure that each small 'parcel' is properly allocated to the individual plan-holder, and that it receives its correct portion of interest due, dividend receipts and tax credits.

In addition, the manager is responsible for all paperwork – both in relation to the stock market and the Inland Revenue. He must supply annual reports and accounts to every plan-holder for each company in which he has a beneficial interest, and is also obliged to provide regular statements concerning his individual account, which must detail every transaction done on his behalf. If the plan-holder wishes to attend a company's annual general meeting, the manager must arrange this for him (though most, as a deterrent, will charge heavily for doing so).

Obviously most of these tasks are computerised. Nonetheless, they are expensive to administer – and virtually guarantee that a PEP manager will lose money in the early years of the scheme. As a final insult, even when a plan-holder has eventually reached the point where he might be profitable to his manager, he is entirely free to up sticks and take his business elsewhere! It's probably true to say that a PEP manager has to work harder for his money than any other type of fund manager – and yet, in the majority of cases, his charges are substantially less. All told, it is hardly surprising that the scheme is not universally popular in the City of London.

## CHARGES

The first financial hurdle for the PEP investor, logically enough, is the *initial* charge levied when his plan is set up. This ranges from an astonishing nil, up to 5% of the value of the investment. The latter is quite common, and no higher than the initial charge levied by unit trusts, but in PEP terms it is uncompetitive. There is a good choice of major schemes charging only 1 to 1.25%, some of which will allow the plan-holder to pay the fee in excess of his PEP contribution.

More important, for long-term PEP investors, is the *annual* charge on the plan's value. A small minority of plan managers (including Barclays) charge only a flat rate – which is probably ideal for larger PEP holders going all-out for capital growth. Most, though, levy another percentage charge on the annual value of the fund – ranging from 0.75 to 2.5% (the most common rates are again 1 to 1.25%). While there's little point in getting over-excited about a fraction of a percentage point, the highest annual rates are best avoided. In later years, they may add very appreciably to the cost.

Any plan manager buying shares on your behalf will incur *dealing costs,* and most pass these on. In most discretionary plans dealing costs are extremely low (typically 0.2% of the value of the deal) – reflecting the buying muscle of the big institutions since the 'Big Bang', in October 1986, deregulated the stock market. Some non-discretionary plans still charge at the old minimum commission rate of 1.65%, though most offer some sort of discount. A typical commission rate is 1.5%, while 0.75% is generous.

Finally, there are any manner of miscellaneous costs – varying immensely from scheme to scheme. Some managers charge a hefty £50 for 'early' withdrawals during the first two years of a plan's life, others charge nothing. Some have small costs associated with 'excessive' switching of investments, or for holding more than three or four shares in any one plan. Only one or two managers charge (lightly) for sending out annual reports, though many discourage plan-holders from attending company meetings. You can always insist on this right – but one manager will hit you for £120 a time!

## KEEPING YOU POSTED

As an absolute minimum, any plan-holder can expect to receive an annual statement of his position – showing the value of his PEP, the shares and other investments in which it is invested, dividends and tax credits received, and details of all transactions done. In addition, he will receive the annual reports and accounts of all companies in his plan, and fund managers' reports on the performance of his unit trusts.

In practice, many plan managers have gone much further than this. Barclays, for example, are prepared to send out monthly statements and all contract notes on deals – complete, in the case of discretionary plans, with an explanation for the manager's investment decision. Fidelity not only supplies regular newsletters, but allows plan-holders to ring in on a freefone line with any queries. Many non-discretionary managers will give dealing recommendations for the shares on their lists. All told, there seems to be a real willingness on the part of many PEP managers to keep their clients well informed and interested in the progress of their investments. PEP investors who genuinely wish to learn more about the stock market should certainly take advantage of the fact.

## INVESTOR PROTECTION

Though a great deal of fuss is made about investor protection, it is very rare indeed for people investing through fund management vehicles to become the victims of fraud. Nonetheless, just in case disaster should strike, it may be worth knowing how the new regulatory framework will affect PEPs.

Since the second half of 1987, when the Financial Services Act came into force, PEPs have come under the ultimate jurisdiction of the Securities and Investments Board (or SIB), which oversees all investment business in the UK (apart from Lloyds). Under the SIB come various Self-Regulating Organisations (or SROs), which police their own patches of the City jungle. Before they can offer PEPs to the public, plan managers now have to be accredited by their SRO (or the SIB itself) as well as by the Inland Revenue. From the PEP investor's point of view, the relevant SROs are TSA (The Securities Association), FIMBRA (Financial Intermediaries, Managers and Brokers Regulatory Association), or IMRO (Investment Managers Regulatory Organisation). These bodies will investigate any complaints against member firms if an investor's direct approach proves unsatisfactory, and are authorised to arbitrate on disputes. In addition, all SROs contribute to a central compensation fund which can be used to reimburse the victims of fraud or financial collapse.

In practice, the PEP investor is in infinitely more danger of a stock market reverse, or even incompetent fund management, than he is from fraud. If the possibility seriously worries you, stick only to large and well-known institutions of unimpeachable integrity.

# 5. Getting the most out of your PEP

## CHOOSING A PEP MANAGER

It is a fact of life that the majority of people buy financial services – like most other things – as a direct result of effective marketing. There is no reason to assume that PEPs have been any different. Rather than try to weigh up the pros and cons of different schemes, most existing plan-holders will have simply answered the most attractive mailshot, or picked up a brochure from their usual bank branch.

Nonetheless, it should be clear by now that PEPs differ enormously – in the scope they offer the investor to make his own investment decisions, in the spread of risk they can accommodate, and in the charges they levy. In practice, if you're to have a good chance of making a PEP work the way *you* want it to, you will have to devote some care at the outset to choosing an appropriate plan manager.

For many people, the selection process will be relatively easy. If you insist upon making all your own investment decisions without restriction, then your choice is currently very narrow. If you want a unit trust only arrangement, you can decide on the basis of performance alone. Then again, there will be specialist concerns. The existing share-holder who switches regularly between blue chips, for example, should look primarily for a non-discretionary scheme with the lowest dealing charges. The man who wants to work at his investment will require one of the more flexible PEPs, allowing a decent range of individual share-holdings and a variety of unit trusts. High-rate taxpayers, investing for growth elsewhere, may wish to select a scheme using every available loophole to boost income.

Decisions concerning discretionary portfolios depend on two crucial factors – performance and suitability. At present, unfortunately, the former involves a considerable amount of guess-work – though it's a reasonable bet that most managers investing in only three or four shares will compensate for the narrow spread by picking very dull companies. Nonetheless, some plan managers profess to be following a high-growth policy, while others concentrate on an above-average yield. The choice here really is important. A basic-rate taxpayer attempting to build up capital over the long term should certainly go for growth – if his plan manager is successful, his tax concession will eventually come in the form of CGT relief. By the same token, high-rate taxpayers approaching retirement – or even those expecting to withdraw their funds as soon as each plan matures – will probably be more interested in income. Clearly, you will not get the best out of your PEP if you pick a plan concentrating on the 'wrong' relief for your own financial circumstances.

No one should invest in a plan without giving some consideration to the charges involved. Unless there seems to be some other (and pretty overwhelming) advantage in their favour, it seems reasonable to reject schemes whose charges are substantially above the norm. Equally, if you intend to build up a substantial fund over the long term, you might well be biased towards schemes offering an unusually low annual charge. In most cases, though, it will not pay to be too finicky. Average initial and annual charges of 1 to 1.25% are entirely reasonable – and in practice, that extra quarter of a percentage point may be well worth paying in return for additional flexibility or feed-back of information. It will certainly be worth paying many times over if it buys superior investment performance in a discretionary plan.

It's clear that the options for PEP investors are still rapidly growing. In addition, many of the figures and scheme details mentioned in this book may be out of date. The Stock Exchange, however, publishes a regular guide to the various plans generally available, and intermediaries Chase de Vere produce a free *Pepsguide* brochure on a monthly basis.

## COPING WITH BEAR MARKETS

One valid criticism of PEPs is that they fail to provide adequate protection against a relapse in the market known as a 'Bear market'. (A rising market is a 'Bull market'.) While the investor outside can simply turn all his holdings into cash, the PEP investor cannot follow suit without losing his tax concessions. So must he just resign himself to riding out the storm? If he's in a discretionary scheme, unfortunately, the answer must be yes – at least there's no alternative to relying on the plan manager's investment skills to mitigate the effects. Non-discretionary plan-holders, however, should be in a position to take defensive steps.

The main weapons in the war against a Bear market are the cash and unit trust concessions. Naturally, in these circumstances, you will want to make sure that your 10% cash entitlement is utilised to the full. The 25% unit trust allowance, however, may be much more important. Provided the Bear market is confined to the UK, you can then park these funds in Japan (or wherever) until domestic conditions look more promising. Even if the downturn is an international phenomenon, there should still be scope to switch into unit trusts investing in defensive sectors like property, or even in 'contra-cyclical' ones like natural resources. The same principle can be applied to your equity holdings. Bear markets are seldom monolithic, with everything falling at once. At the beginning of the 1980–81 recession, for example, both the electronics and natural resources sectors performed strongly, while engineers and other traditional manufacturers crashed. The sun never goes in for everybody. During the recession, the sky-high levels of both the pound and interest rates hurt most companies badly – but they certainly didn't do any harm to importers and firms with large sums on deposit. Though it is not easy to make money during a Bear market unless your investment skills are unusually well developed, it should at least be possible to limit your losses.

Naturally, these techniques are only possible within a reasonably flexible non-discretionary plan. And they do suggest that it is always a good idea to preserve your holdings in unit trusts. Remember, once they've been switched into equities, they cannot be switched back again.

The man holding only part of his portfolio in a PEP, of course, is in a much more favourable position. Few investors move completely into cash during a Bear phase – even if they scale down heavily, most keep a few shares on the boil just in case the market stages a sudden recovery. By moving completely into cash outside his PEP, and retaining his shares inside it, the stock market investor keeps both his tax concessions and his 'presence' in the market. His *overall* risk, of course, will be much reduced.

## BALANCED INVESTMENT

As a general rule of stock market investment, risk and reward are two sides of the same coin. If you buy into just one company, you will do extremely well if it prospers, extremely badly if it fails. This may not bother you if you're of a speculative bent – some people positively enjoy chancing their arm. But if your PEP is designed to serve a serious investment purpose, it is a thoroughly unsatisfactory approach.

The wider your 'spread' of investments, the lower your risk – any shares turning sour will be offset by those doing unusually well. By the same token, of course, your chances of outperforming the market by a wide margin are also reduced. If you held a hundred or more large companies in your portfolio (which isn't really feasible for private investors), you would probably perform exactly in line with the market average. Most private investors aim to have somewhere between 10 and 20 shares in their portfolio – towards the lower end if they are going all-out for growth, rather higher if risk-avoidance is a major concern.

How does this fit in with the PEPs available? At first glance, not very well. Only Lloyds and the Prudential allow a truly comprehensive spread, though quite a few schemes offer a limit of eight to ten shares in any one PEP – just about adequate, but still too concentrated for many tastes. Many others limit planholders to three or four shares, or even fewer. Of course, this need not matter to investors with existing portfolios – looking at their share-holdings in the round, they should still have an adequate spread. But if your PEP represents your first foray on to the stock market, you should make a point of avoiding schemes which are too narrowly based. Find one offering eight to ten shares in addition to a full allocation of unit or investment trusts, and you can feel reasonably confident. Planholders contributing less than £1,680 a year are best advised to select a scheme which puts the first £420 into unit trusts automatically – as this will increase the proportion of funds securely housed.

The narrow spread problem has come in for considerable comment from critics of the PEP scheme, but it's important to keep matters in perspective. Many existing investors on the stock market, after all, couldn't afford to start off with a fully-fledged portfolio – they build it up, share by share, over a period. In this regard, some PEPs can even be regarded as helpful – for even if you had the full £2,400 to invest, you wouldn't be able to buy more than four shares in the normal way without incurring very heavy dealing costs. It tends to be forgotten that many people of relatively modest means actually *want* to play the stock market and not be nannied by fund managers. Thanks to PEPs, this is now feasible.

In addition, it is all too easy to regard any one plan in isolation, treating the £2,400 limit as permanent rather than annual. If you intend to open a new plan each year, it obviously won't take long to broaden your portfolio into its desired shape. Obviously, in a non-discretionary plan, there is no need to go on buying the same shares. Even a highly restrictive scheme, limiting you to three shares per plan, will allow you to build up a decent portfolio over three or four years. Nor should it be forgotten that many of the restrictions currently associated with PEPs stem from their extreme youth. Once funds grow larger, and become more profitable to manage, it is likely that most of them will also become much more flexible. In these conditions, plan-holders should be able to adopt their ideal investment profile much more quickly.

There is, however, more to balanced investment than mere numbers of shares. On the whole, it is a very poor investment policy to concentrate all your holdings in the same sectors of the market – banks, say, or electronic companies. Sometimes industries suffer their own private recessions, and companies involved in them find their share prices falling across the board. Many private investors, for example, were dazzled by high-technology companies in the early 1980s – investing in little else. They were badly burned when the sector turned down in 1985, though the market as a whole remained strong. Equally, the element of fashion on the stock market should never be forgotten. Invest only in takeover situations or recovery stocks, and you may be left high and dry if enthusiasms move elsewhere.

As a rule, then, it pays to have your fingers in several different pies. If your plan is discretionary, you must rely on your plan manager to take care of this for you. If non-discretionary, you can slowly improve the balance of your portfolio as the number of shareholdings build up. Many non-discretionary plans provide a brief potted description of the companies in their list – and even if they don't, it is not difficult to find the necessary information elsewhere.

# 6. Equities and how they are traded

## WHAT SHARES ARE

Put money in the building society, buy National Savings
Certificates, invest in Government gilt-edged securities or corporate bonds, and you are lending money in return for the
promise of interest. Your capital is ultimately secure (unless the
borrower goes bust), though the trading price of marketable
debt securities will fluctuate according to supply and demand.

Ordinary shares, or equities, are quite different. They represent capital, not debt, and confer nothing but part-ownership of
a company. Collectively, share-holders own the company – its
assets and its profits – but are not guaranteed any return
whatsoever. If the business booms, the share-holders will profit
handsomely. If it goes bust, they will be last in line for any
repayment.

The idea of shared equity developed centuries ago. Rather
than put all their eggs in one basket, merchants often decided to
pool their risks in different enterprises. One might, for example, buy an eighth share of a ship trading with the Levant, and a
quarter share of another business insuring cargoes. If the
ventures proved successful, the profits would be shared out *pro
rata* among the owners. Should any of them find a more
promising use for their capital, they would be able to sell their
'share' of the business on to other businessmen. Naturally, the
development of this system allowed businesses to raise capital
far beyond the means of any single investor.

The same principles still apply – with one crucial difference.
Originally, owners were not just entitled to a share of the
profits, they also had unlimited liability to meet their share of
the business's debts. These days, most companies (certainly all
companies quoted on The Stock Exchange) are *limited* com-

panies. Share-holders can still lose their entire investment if a company goes bankrupt, but they are not personally liable for the company's debts.

We do not talk any more about 'one-eighth' or 'one-quarter' shares. Modern companies divide their capital into millions of shares, each of which represents such a minute fraction of the whole, that the actual figure is difficult to comprehend. Nonetheless, this remains the reality behind all share ownership. If a company has ten million shares in issue, then each one represents one ten-millionth of the business. Buy 1,000 of these tiny particles of capital, and you own one ten-thousandth of the company's assets and profits.

Share-holders take the risks, and reap the rewards. In this regard, they are no different from house owners. If you buy a £50,000 house with a £40,000 mortgage, your equity stake is £10,000. If the house doubles in price, your equity is worth six times as much – £60,000. If it halves, your equity is worth nothing – for the mortgagor has first charge. Similarly with companies. Trade creditors, bank lenders and loan stock holders are all first in the queue. Only after everyone else has been satisfied does the ordinary share-holder get a look in. Nonetheless, he should still be the biggest winner if the business does well – for once a company's liabilities have been met, the share-holder is entitled to everything else.

## HOW SHARES WORK

Owning part of a business is all very well, but how can you expect to profit thereby? If you buy into a tiny chain of shops, and it develops into the Marks and Spencers of tomorrow, how will this massively-enhanced value be transmitted to the share-holders?

Essentially, in two ways. That bigger business will be earning far larger profits than before, and out of those profits it will pay larger dividends to its share-holders. In addition, since each share will represent an equal fraction of a much larger and more valuable business, other investors will be prepared to pay more for it – its price will rise on the stock market. Ultimately, the value of a share is completely at the mercy of supply and demand – you will never get more for it than someone else is willing to pay. Even so, investors are not just playing a blind-folded game of pass the parcel. A share's real worth can be assessed according to three criteria.

## Dividends

All a company can promise its share-holders is to let them participate in its profits. Accordingly, it pays out a portion of its annual profits (usually twice-yearly) in the form of dividends. As profits rise, so should the dividends rise in tandem. Naturally, over the longer term, a share's value should increase with the income flow it is producing. Companies declare dividends in pence per share, net of tax at the basic rate. By applying this figure to the current share price, it is then possible to calculate a 'yield', comparable to the interest paid out on other forms of investment.

Yields are usually quoted 'gross', which means that the net dividend figure has to be adjusted for the basic-rate tax deduction. This allows investors to calculate their own real return according to their particular marginal rate of tax – though for PEP purposes, the gross yield is obviously the true one. The 'grossing up' formula is quite simple – with a basic rate of 27%, you simply multiply the dividend by 100, then divide by 73. If tax falls to 25%, you multiply by 100, then divide by 75.

The gross dividend, expressed as a percentage of the share price, is its yield. If a company's shares are priced at 100p, and it declares a net dividend of 5p (i.e. a gross dividend of 6.85p), its yield is 6.85%. These yields, of course, are supplied ready-made in the papers – though they are calculated to the latest share price and are therefore constantly fluctuating. If prices rise faster than dividends, yields will appear to fall.

From the investor's point of view, however, yields should normally be on an upward trend – for the price actually paid for a share does not alter. Suppose you bought shares in that company at 100p, initially yielding 6.85%. If the price stays the same, yet dividends increase by 10% a year, the yield after five years will be 11% – and after ten years, nearly 18%. These, of course, are exceptionally high figures – and in practice, the shares would have risen over the intervening period as the dividend flow became more valuable.

## Earnings

If a company is to expand, it must invest. If it distributes all its profits to share-holders, it will only be able to do so by borrowing – in which case, the interest on its debt will reduce future profits. In practice, therefore, most companies pay out only a fraction of their profits in the form of dividends. The rest is ploughed back into the business.

There is no need for share-holders to feel cheated. The more a company invests, the faster its profits – and dividends – should grow in future. For that reason, investors do not just look at current dividends. They also look at a company's earnings as an indication of the future dividend flow.

When a company announces its results every six months, it usually publishes several figures. The most important of these are its sales, its profits before tax, the dividend per share and – possibly most interesting of all – the earnings per share (often abbreviated to eps). The latter is based on profits after tax and all other deductions (attributable profits) – and represents the highest dividend the company could have paid without dipping into its reserves. The difference between the eps and dividend figure is the amount, per share, the company is reinvesting to develop the business. Collectively, these are known as 'retained profits'.

In practice, equity investors are usually more interested in earnings than in dividends – even though the reward from them is less tangible. The reason for this is simple. If all you want is an immediate return on your investment, you can almost always obtain a far higher yield from a building society account (or National Savings Certificates or gilts) than you will get from shares. Share-holders are primarily after capital and dividend *growth* – and for that they require their companies to become larger and more profitable. The growth in a company's earnings is a far more reliable indicator of its real progress than the dividend payments.

Earnings per share are used to calculate a share's PE ratio. This is normally by far the most important yardstick used by investors to judge whether a share is a good investment or not – and we will examine it in detail in Chapter 7.

## Assets

A share does not merely confer a tiny portion of a company's profits. Ownership of a business includes everything the business itself owns – its factories, stocks, outstanding bills (debtors) and cash holdings – even its patents and trademarks. Collectively, these items are known as the company's assets. Divide the value of these assets among the shares in issue, and the result is an assets per share figure. This may stand above or (more commonly) below the prevailing share price.

Assets should grow roughly in line with profits – or, more strictly, with those 'retained' profits we saw being ploughed back into the business. The cash, after all, may be used to finance a higher level of business activity, or to buy more efficient and valuable equipment, or to build a new factory. In practice, however, things are seldom so simple. Bad management may blow all their retained profits on a disastrous new venture or misconceived promotion campaign. Good management may borrow funds to increase their investment, and earn a higher return for their share-holders than the interest cost of this additional finance.

Though they own the assets, share-holders will not normally see any direct benefit from them – everything depends on how successfully the assets are utilised to produce profits and dividends. The key word, though, is 'normally'. In practice, if a share price falls far below its asset backing, the company may well attract a takeover bid. In the corporate jungle, there are plenty of predators on the prowl for 'cheap' assets – usually to be found among the market's weaker and least profitable brethren. For this reason, shares still have a value even if the company is making losses and paying nothing in dividends. Sooner or later, share-holders can hope that the assets will come to their rescue.

# HOW THE STOCK MARKET WORKS

If the only thing that mattered were dividends, and if share-holders were content to stick with the same investments for ever, there would be no need for a stock market. Companies could raise any capital they needed direct from the public, and that would be the end of the matter.

Of course, neither of these conditions holds good. As we have seen, most investors are more interested in capital growth than in dividends – and for this to be realised, they need access to third parties prepared to take shares off their hands. At the same time, no one wishes to be committed to the same investments for ever. Individual companies rise and fall, more interesting opportunities turn up, cash may be needed for some completely different purpose. In reality, companies can only raise capital from the public if their shares are (or will be) freely traded. In other words, there has to be a market.

The functions of the stock market are therefore twofold. Its 'primary' (and economically most valuable) function is to provide an organised venue for companies seeking to raise new capital. Companies making an offer for sale direct to the public first have to satisfy The Stock Exchange that their shares are suitable for trading. Capital-raising, though, need not be a one-off event. Many established companies issue additional shares to fund their development – either through 'rights issues' to existing share-holders or (on a limited scale) 'placings' with selected institutions. None of these things would be possible without the market's 'secondary' function – giving the original providers of capital the opportunity to sell their shares on to other investors. In practice – since there are obviously far more established companies than new ones – this trade in second-hand shares predominates.

The origins of the stock market are ordinary enough. Back in the seventeenth century, anyone interested in investing in shares would go to one of the City coffee houses specialising in this sort of business (others, including Lloyd's, handled insurance, or shipping, or letters of credit). In the coffee houses, details of new ventures wishing to raise capital would be posted, and buyers and sellers of shares in existing companies could be introduced. Later on, the despised 'stockjobbers' emerged – street-traders who set up their share-dealing stalls at suitable vantage points in the City, and who often tricked unwary members of the public into investing in wholly fictitious enterprises.

The modern Stock Exchange is an infinitely more sophisticated affair. It controls the conduct of its members, who are alone accredited to deal in shares in public companies, and tries to ensure that all dealings on the market are fair and orderly. In addition, there are stringent rules governing companies allowed a 'listing' on the exchange. Directors dealing in their own company's shares are restricted to certain periods, and minimum reporting requirements are laid down. All dealing and settlement procedures are according to Stock Exchange rules, and must be channelled through centralised systems administered by the Exchange's officials.

Before the 'Big Bang' (October 1986), The Stock Exchange used to maintain a rigid distinction between two types of members – jobbers, who dealt in shares as principals on their own account, and stockbrokers, who were confined to acting as agents for the public. Many specialist (or 'agency') stockbrokers still exist, though most of the biggest City firms now combine the broking and jobbing functions. In the second capacity, they are known as 'market-makers' – and it is these market-makers, like the jobbers of old, who 'make' prices in shares.

Prices don't just come out of the blue, as the result of some dealer's whim. Unlike investors, market-makers are not dealing in shares for their long-term potential – they are trying to make a cut out of two-way business, just like any other trader. In other words, they want both buyers *and* sellers – and for the most part, they want them as equally matched as possible. Shares bought and left on a dealer's book have to be financed (just like a shopkeeper's stock), while shares sold have to be procured in order that the dealer can meet his commitments.

It is the market-maker's constant manoeuvring to keep his book balanced which moves share prices. Suppose a company, whose shares are priced at 100p, announces some unexpectedly bad news. Some investors will undoubtedly sell out – and the market-maker will take the shares on his book. In the circumstances, it is most unlikely that he will find buyers prepared to take these shares off his hands at anything like 100p. He must therefore drop the price until other investors think the shares are worth buying. If he drops it too far, investors will buy more shares than he has available, and he will then have to raise the price until he attracts further selling. Eventually, he will find a 'level' at which buying and selling is more or less matched.

In practice, needless to say, the process is nothing like so crude. Market-makers often anticipate what investors are going to do – and in the example given above, would almost certainly have lowered the price from 100p before anyone had a chance to sell. Moreover, the price adjustments are well-nigh continuous – virtually any large transaction, unless immediately matched by another in the opposite direction, will have the market-makers tinkering with their prices – up 2p one minute, down 3p the next. The essential point, though, is that prices are ultimately set by supply and demand – and by that alone. The market-maker doesn't care two hoots whether a share looks cheap or expensive. All he is trying to do when he adjusts his prices is to get buyers and sellers roughly in balance – for the more successfully he does so, the more money he will make. As a mechanism for ensuring that prices accurately and impartially reflect the day-to-day state of supply and demand, the stock market is undeniably efficient. Infinitely more so, say, than the housing, art or used car markets.

## HOW SHARES ARE TRADED

Before the Big Bang, the vast bulk of deals were done on the 'floor' of The Stock Exchange. The jobbers, forerunners of today's market-makers, stood at their hexagonal pitches making their various prices, and brokers moved among them seeking the best prices on offer for their clients.

Far sooner than anyone expected, the floor has become redundant – virtually all dealings are now done between offices. These days, when you (or your PEP manager) puts in an order for shares, the broker will simply call up the company in question on his computer terminal. With the introduction of SEAQ (Stock Exchange Automated Quotation system), the market-makers key in their prices direct, which are then displayed on the screen.

In the previous section, we discussed a share priced at 100p. What the broker actually sees, though, is a range of prices. In this case, if three market-makers are dealing in the share, he might find one offering 98-101p, another 97-100p, and the third 99-102p. In each set, the lower of the two prices is the market-maker's buying price, the higher his selling price. The difference between the two (the 'spread' or 'turn') represents his dealing profit. The screen will also display the most favourable prices for investors – in this case, 99-100p. If a broker is transacting a 'sell' order, he will go to the third market-maker who is offering to buy shares at 99p. If he wants to buy, he will go to the second who is offering to sell at 100p. If the broker and the market-maker belong to the same firm, a potential conflict of interest obviously arises. Stock Exchange rules forbid brokers to deal in-house unless their own firm is offering the keenest price available.

Why do the prices differ? As we have already seen, market-makers adjust their prices according to the state of their 'book'. In this case, the man offering 99-102p will attract all the selling orders, and no buying orders – so he will be a net buyer of shares. This is almost certainly deliberate – it may be that an hour earlier he sold a large number which he must now obtain from the market. As soon as his book is back in balance, he will move his prices down in line with the others. Market-makers, then, are constantly manoeuvring around each other – even when a price is basically static. Naturally, if a substantial shift in supply/demand occurs, all three will move their prices up or down to compensate.

Once you have placed an order with a broker, orally or not, you are committed. Having checked the prices, the broker will phone the relevant market-maker and do the deal – both the broker (who is responsible for his client) and the market-maker are then also committed. A couple of days later (if you are dealing on your own account) you can expect to receive a contract note. This will give details of the number of shares dealt, the price, the 'consideration' (or cost of the shares) and the dealing charges. Until the share certificate arrives (which may take several weeks), the contract note is proof of ownership.

Though you own shares from the moment your order is transacted, you do not have to pay for them immediately. Unlike most of the world's stock markets, The London Stock Exchange operates on an account system. Each account lasts for two (or occasionally three) weeks – and all deals transacted within a single account are later settled simultaneously. The back-room boys in brokers' and market-makers' offices agree what deals have been done at the end of each trading day, and all buy and sell notes are then fed into The Stock Exchange's settlement system (Talisman). This effectively sorts out precisely who owes what shares to whom at the end of the account. Not until Settlement day (ten days after the end of the account), are cash payments due. Brokers send out statements to their clients, detailing their transactions during the account – accompanied by a cheque if any monies are due. Otherwise, statements act as a bill, with clients expected to settle up as soon as possible. One big advantage of the account system is that it requires only one payment. No matter how many deals you have done during the account period, all proceeds from sales will be offset against purchases.

The settlement system is reasonably efficient, though the huge increase in dealing volumes which followed the Big Bang put it under some strain. From the private investor's point of view, it is reasonably simple to understand – but the paperwork can be tiresome. Apart from checking contract notes (which normally have to be retained for tax purposes), and settling up on Settlement day, anyone selling shares has to fill in a transfer certificate and return it to his broker. One of the advantages of the PEP scheme, of course, is that all this paperwork will be handled by your plan manager. If administrative efficiency is not your *forte*, it helps to justify his charges.

# 7. The thrills and spills of investment

As we saw in the previous chapter, anyone dealing in shares can be sure of a price which fairly reflects the state of supply and demand. In terms of where the price will go next, that provides no guarantees whatsoever. Supply and demand fluctuates constantly on the stock market – and necessarily so, if you want your investments to be successful. When you buy a share, it is in the hope that investors coming after you will be prepared to pay more for it. At the same time, you run the risk that they will pay less.

## BULL AND BEAR MARKETS

No share can be considered in isolation – it will usually be affected, to a greater or lesser extent, by investors' attitudes to the stock market as a whole. This, in turn, reflects economic reality. When the economy is booming, most companies naturally prosper. When recession strikes, most of them have to contend with falling profits, many get into financial difficulties, and a few go under.

As everyone knows, the economy moves in cycles – recession inexorably following expansion, and *vice versa*. The stock market reflects these economic changes – or, to be more accurate, tries to anticipate them – and so share prices, too, move in cycles. When prices are moving ahead across the board, shares are said to be in a Bull market. When falling, they are in a Bear market. Apply these expressions to individual investors, and a 'Bull' is an optimist or buyer of shares, a 'Bear' a pessimist or seller.

The Bull market of the mid-1980s has been one of the longest and biggest on record (see Fig. 5). Precisely when it began is a

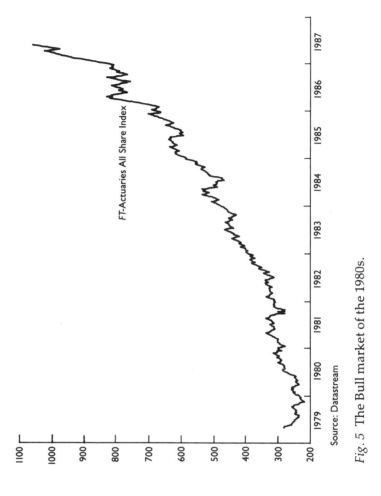

Fig. 5 The Bull market of the 1980s.

matter of some dispute (a major change of market direction is only obvious long after the event), though many chart its beginnings back to the autumn of 1981. That was the year, interestingly enough, when traditional British manufacturing industry plumbed the nadir of the recession – factories were closing almost daily, and the dole queues were lengthening with unprecedented speed. Why, then, should share prices have begun to ease slowly ahead? Remember that the stock market is all about anticipation. By 1981, prices in many British companies had already fallen substantially. Cannier investors realised as early as 1979 that the policies of the new Tory administration were going to put industry through the wringer – and the evidence of impending recession was steadily gathering force in the early months of 1980. That year, share prices in companies vulnerable to an economic downturn fell heavily.

But why should investors suddenly change their minds in 1981? The truth is, most of them didn't. After prices have been falling for a considerable time, there comes a point when remaining share-holders feel they might as well hang on for conditions to improve. As the 'supply' of shares from sellers dries up, so prices begin to stabilise – encouraging a few bargain-hunters to re-enter the market. In 1981, of course, the country's economic prospects still looked very bleak. Nonetheless, optimists could argue that the bad times would not last for ever – and that British industry (or as much of it as survived) would eventually emerge much leaner, fitter and more profitable from its trial.

As events have proved, these early birds were correct – though real evidence of economic recovery didn't start emerging until 1983. Most investors, naturally, hold off until favourable news starts coming through – and then invest in greater and greater numbers as confidence mounts. Bull markets, then, gather momentum as they progress. Only since 1983 has the latest example been blatantly apparent to one and all. Each year since then, it has appeared to gain in strength.

If Bull markets often start when the news seems darkest, Bear markets have a tendency to develop when the economy is booming. Again it is all a matter of anticipation. Investors know that economic expansion does not continue without interruptions, and that setbacks are inevitable. After a Bull market has been running for some time, many of them are sitting on substantial profits and do not want to lose them in the next downturn. Eventually, then, the buying tends to dry up and some scattered selling emerges. If prices continue to rise (and sometimes, at the end of a Bull market, they rise very steeply), it is usually on a dwindling volume of trading.

We have already seen that many investors started selling in 1979 and early 1980 – a period when the economy seemed to be muddling through reasonably well, and a Tory Government (always to the market's liking) had just been elected. But if shares in traditional manufacturing companies fell, it was not possible to claim that the whole market was in a Bear phase. At the same time, natural resources companies were booming (the second great hike in oil prices occurred in 1979), and investors were also getting excited about the possibilities of the microchip and the increased importance of service industries. Overall, the market – at least as measured by the major indices – was basically flat.

For the last real Bear market, we have to go all the way back to 1973–74. In the traditional manner, the previous Bull market had gradually conked out as inventors wondered how long the boom of the early 1970s could last. At that time, economic expansion always ended up by 'overheating' – inflationary bottlenecks emerging as spare labour and productive capacity reached their limits. For most of 1973, equities suffered a mild Bear market against the background of a still growing economy. What really set the cat among the pigeons was the first oil crisis which followed the Yom Kippur War.

The oil crisis set in motion a series of disastrous events. Shortage of energy supplies forced the Government to stamp down on business activity by withdrawing liquidity from the economy. That, in turn, caused the previously booming property market to dry up. Property developers went bankrupt, taking with them many of the 'fringe' banks which had financed their activities. Major financial institutions, which had lent huge sums to the fringe banks, also became suspect. In no time at all, a massive crisis of financial confidence developed. If that weren't bad enough, the miners' strike of early 1974 toppled the Government, and led to the election of a left-wing administration hostile to the City in general, and the stock market in particular. Figure 6 shows how quickly investor unease developed into panic, and finally into complete despair.

The Bear Market of 1973–74 was freakishly bad – a complete collapse of confidence which, according to the experts, can be expected once every 50 years or so. It is worth remembering, too, that it came at the beginning of a severe dislocation of the world economy, for escalating energy prices kept inflation high, and growth low, for the remainder of the decade. It can equally be argued, of course, that the great Bull market of the mid-1980s has been freakishly good. This may well be so. The period has witnessed a huge fall in energy prices in real terms, not to mention a 'second industrial revolution' as the new microchip technology has been applied to an ever-wider range of industries. Around the world, inflation has been brought under control – while in the UK, many of the chronic problems

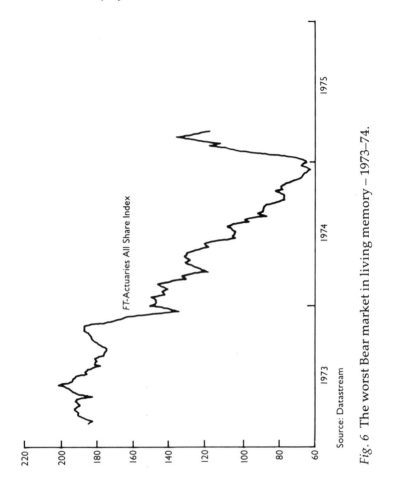

FT-Actuaries All Share Index

Source: Datastream

*Fig. 6* The worst Bear market in living memory – 1973–74.

dogging manufacturing industry (feeble management, over-manning and militant unionism) have improved substantially.

One can only speculate what future Bull and Bear markets will look like. According to one school of thought, the huge rise in prices of the early 1980s must – eventually – produce an equally severe reaction. According to another, there may be a reversion to the 'classic' cycles of the 1950s and early 1960s – relatively unspectacular Bull markets lasting roughly two years, interspersed by year-long Bear markets when shares lose roughly a third of previous gains. The truth is, nobody knows – all comment about where the market is going (in anything but the shortest term) is essentially guesswork. Whatever happens in future, however, key features of market behaviour are likely to hold good. Markets hate uncertainty (whether political or economic), they are always trying to anticipate events – and they always exaggerate. Prospects are never so rosy as a rip-roaring Bull might suggest, or as bleak as they seem in the lowest depths of a Bear market. Long-term investors who pick their shares wisely, who switch into 'defensive' sectors when the going gets really tough, and who can avoid the emotional extremes of euphoria and panic, should ride out the occasional storms without too much damage.

## INDIVIDUAL SHARE MOVEMENTS

A tremendous amount of speculation is lavished on where the market is going next – the 'market' in this context meaning the main market indices. In the end, though, these merely measure an agglomeration of individual share price movements. They may tell you what is happening to the 'average' share, even to most shares, but no more.

In reality, individual shares do their own thing. Look at a list of share prices on a 'bad' day for the market, and you will always find many which haven't moved, and a few which have gone up against the trend. We have already seen how, at the beginning of the decade, shares behaved in radically different ways – oil, electronics and service companies generally prospered, manufacturing companies fell steeply. Investors, after all, do not buy the 'market' – or, for that matter, the economy. They buy shares in individual companies with individual business prospects. In a recession, when business is difficult, most companies may be adversely affected. But there are always the exceptions – companies with the good fortune to be in growing niche markets, for example, or those run by exceptionally determined and adaptable management. Equally, of course, some companies contrive to do badly even in the most favourable economic conditions.

As with the market as a whole, investors are always looking towards a company's future. No matter that the business performed brilliantly in the past, and is doing badly today. As a new shareholder, your return depends on the profits to come, and the dividends they will provide.

The future, in business as in anything else, is far from certain.

Investors need to form a 'view' of a company's prospects, and however well or ill-informed that view may be, it must always involve an element of guesswork. In these circumstances, it is rare that there will ever be a complete consensus. Remember that for everyone buying a share at a given price, there will be others selling.

So the right price for a share is only a matter of opinion? Ultimately, the answer must be yes. But the stock market represents thousands of conflicting opinions. What matters – what actually shifts prices – is the *balance* of market opinion. If more buyers think a share is cheap than sellers think it expensive, then it will rise.

Though opinion about a company is influenced by many things, the most important factor is usually investors' view of the next year's profits. When a company announces its profits for the year, it may have only a vague idea how it will perform in the following period. Stockbrokers' analysts, however, will weigh up the various factors involved in the company's business, and produce a profit forecast. For want of anything else, most investors will probably take this as a reliable indication – though others may feel on various grounds that the analyst has been too cautious or too optimistic. As the year progresses, more dependable indicators of progress will come to light – most importantly, the interim (or half-yearly) results. At the same time, variables which affect profits (exchange rates, interest rates, levels of consumer spending and so forth) will be better known. Analysts often change their forecasts during the course of a company's year – though they often disagree with each other, and in the end they may all be wide of the mark. In the press, you will often see the comment that a company's profits were 'higher (or lower) than expected'.

As these expectations change, or are confirmed or disproved, so demand for a share will change. Suppose buyers and sellers are roughly in balance at a price of 100p, the consensus being that the company will make profits of £20m. Should analysts later change their minds (say, for example, the company has managed to secure some bumper orders), they might amend their forecasts to around £30m. Given these much-improved prospects, would-be sellers (at 100p) will probably have second thoughts, while other investors will think the shares look cheap at the price. The supply-demand balance will alter in favour of the Bulls and the price will rise.

Profit expectations may be vitally important, but they are not the only factors influencing opinion. The arrival of new management, a major promotion campaign, even a change of investment fashion, may make a share more or less desirable. One obvious question arises, though – why don't all investors just buy the most promising companies, and ignore the rest? The answer, simply put, is that promising companies cost more than sluggards. Value cannot be measured by the price alone – a share priced at 100p can easily be 'cheaper' than one at 30p. To find out how expensive a share is, it is necessary to crunch a few numbers.

# EVALUATING SHARES

As we saw in the previous chapter, investors are primarily interested in a company's earnings and dividends – and, on occasions, its assets. When these are related to the current share price, they provide several important measurements of value.

## Yield

Gross dividends, expressed as a percentage of the price, give a share's yield. As a yardstick, this is by far the easiest for new investors to assimilate, for the yield can be directly compared with interest rates paid on more familiar investments. As a rule, the comparison is not flattering. Equity yields are currently low (averaging 3.5% at the beginning of 1987) – with only the exceptional share ever coming close to the return paid on gilts or building society accounts.

The crucial difference, of course, is that dividends can normally be expected to increase. Even in years when profits are flat, companies will often sanction a rise so long as they can see better times ahead. Certainly, dividends are only cut when absolutely necessary for the health of the business. Even companies making losses sometimes manage to maintain their payment by dipping into reserves – though this can never be more than a temporary expedient.

Though the average is low, yields vary enormously – while some approach double figures, others are just a fraction of 1%. The reason for the disparity is that low-yielding shares are usually increasing their dividends at a much faster rate – for rapidly expanding companies, an annual rise of 50% or more is not uncommon. Generally speaking (and it can never be more than a generalisation), the higher the yield, the lower the rate of dividend growth. Certainly, investors should be wary of the very highest yields on offer. This often signifies that the market has very low growth expectations – and may even be anticipating a dividend cut.

Traditionally, since the tax regime has strongly favoured capital growth over income, private investors have tended not to pay much attention to yield. It is, even so, easily the most tangible yardstick for measuring a share's value – for unlike most, it represents a real benefit. Eventually, it must put a 'prop' under the share price, for the yield will rise as a price falls (a share yielding 4% at 100p, for example, will yield 8% at 50p). This cannot go on for ever. At some point, a share will yield as much as investments offering a fixed rate of interest. Providing the dividend is 'safe', and has some prospect of increasing, the share will represent a better investment on income grounds alone.

For PEP investors, especially those on high rates of income tax, yield is clearly of much more interest than usual. The important thing to remember, though, is that higher yields generally go hand in hand with slower growth and, ultimately, with smaller capital gains. In equity investment, you can seldom have your cake and eat it.

## Price/earnings ratio

In the last chapter, we met *earnings per share* – a company's annual profits after all deductions, divided by the number of shares in issue.

In the old days, investors used this figure to calculate an earnings yield. If a company priced at 100p, for example, earned 4p and paid a dividend of 3p, it would have an earnings yield of 4% and a dividend yield of 3%. If the shares rose to 200p, the earnings yield would fall to 2%.

Today, earnings yields are obsolete. Instead, investors merely divide the earnings per share figure into the share price to produce a price/earnings (or PE) ratio. A company at 100p earning 4p thus has a PE ratio of 25. The PE is by far the most important yardstick used to measure the value of a share at any given price – particularly its value relative to other shares. Anyone seriously interested in individual share selection cannot afford to ignore it.

All else being equal, the higher the PE (i.e. the lower the earnings yield), the more expensive the share. This is slightly easier to grasp if one considers some alternative expressions for the PE. In the example given above, the 100p shares might be described as '25 times earnings', or on an 'earnings multiple of 25'. This means, in effect, that it will take 25 years' earnings to match the current share price. A share on an earnings multiple (PE) of 10, will take only ten years to earn its price, and must therefore be cheaper.

So why don't all investors simply ignore shares on high PEs, and buy those on low ones? As usual, the answer boils down to expectations. If all shares started off on the same PE (say 15), it wouldn't take long before faster growing companies became much cheaper than the sluggards. If earnings per share double, for example, and the share price remains the same, the PE ratio must halve – in this case, to 7.5. Clearly, it would be nonsensical for a company which looked likely to double earnings in three years to be valued the same as another which might take a decade. Demand for the former will be much greater, forcing up the price – and with it, the PE ratio.

The PE, then, is an effective indicator of the market's growth expectations. As a rough rule of thumb, companies whose shares have a PE in line with the market average can be expected to grow at an average rate. If the PE is much higher than this, it suggests that investors are anticipating rapid growth. Much lower, and the company's performance is expected to be well below par.

One of the main investment skills is deciding whether a company's PE ratio fairly represents its prospects. If, for example, you are pretty sure that a company can raise profits by a quarter each year, and this is considerably higher than the rate expected for company profits generally, you might reasonably consider the shares cheap on an average PE ratio. Often, when commentators discuss companies, they will remark that the shares are 'under-priced' or 'due for a re-rating'. What they usually mean is that the PE is too low.

High PEs may be justified by a company's prospects, but they also spell higher risk. It is essential to remember that the market's expectations can sometimes be over-optimistic –

especially when it is trying to look more than a year into the future. Naturally, the higher expectations are, the greater the scope for disappointment. Should progress fail to come up to scratch for any reason, the effect on the share price is then likely to be disproportionate – for investors will be wary of repeating their mistake. Say, for example, a company priced at 100p is earning 3p per share, and is expected to raise this by 50% to 4.5p in the course of the year. The PE ratio is thus expected to fall from an exceptionally high 33 to around 22 – still well above average, but justified by the excellent growth rate. If, in the event, growth is only 25% to earnings of 3.75p, the implied price for the shares would only be 82.5p (3.75p × 22) – and not even that high if the disappointing results caused the market to downgrade its opinion of the company. It might decide, for example, that a more suitable earnings multiple would now be just a couple of points above the market average – say 17. If so, the implied share price would then be only 64p (17 × 3.75p). In other words, a 25% increase in profits and earnings might be followed by a very substantial fall in the share price.

No amount of 'book-learning' will really teach you how PE ratios operate on share prices – so at the beginning, if you are still feeling your way on the stock market, it is probably safer to stick to moderately-rated companies with more-or-less average prospects. If you follow the market with any care, it shouldn't take too long before the uses and abuses of this crucial yardstick become familiar. At that point, it is reasonably safe to adopt a more adventurous approach.

## Asset backing

In the last chapter, we saw how a company's assets might sometimes underpin the share price – even if profits are non-existent. Takeover specialists pay a great deal of attention to assets, for they often provide a clue that a company could be much more profitable if efficiently managed. Investors who select shares primarily for their asset backing are usually angling for a bid.

Assets per share are found by dividing the assets presented in a company's balance sheet by the number of shares in issue. The resulting figure cannot always be taken at face value, however – companies are allowed a great deal of leeway in presenting their accounts, and balance sheet valuations are occasionally very misleading. You might find, for example, that a company has included the land and buildings it owns at cost price, or at a valuation years out of date. Equally, assets can be overstated. In a recession, especially, industrial property in a hard-hit area is likely to fall in value, while equipment which becomes obsolete may be virtually worthless. People ploughing through balance sheets on the lookout for take-over candidates must normally be prepared to read between the lines.

For certain specialist companies, the assets per share figure is the main valuation yardstick – take-over prospects or no. This applies mainly to investment trusts, property companies and firms involved in oil and mineral exploration. In all three cases, investors are buying shares primarily for the appreciation of the underlying assets – *not* for their earning power. This is most obvious in the first two cases, where investors are using shares in the company to buy into an underlying portfolio of shares or property. In addition, most small exploration companies can only really be assessed according to the value of their discoveries, though producing an asset value in such cases is a highly complicated business. Apart from the assessed value of 'proven' and 'probable' reserves, natural resources companies also own prospecting licenses – the perceived value of which depends on the probability of any discoveries. On the whole, this is a very specialised area, and unsuited to beginners on the stock market.

# TECHNICAL ANALYSIS AND CHARTS

The yardsticks we have been discussing are all concerned with 'fundamental' analysis – the evaluation of a share's real worth in terms of earnings, dividends and assets. All fundamental analysis can do, however, is demonstrate whether a share appears to be cheap or expensive. It can tell you whether a share *ought* to rise or fall, but it cannot dictate price movements.

A totally different approach is 'technical' analysis. This ignores considerations of fundamental value, and tries simply to predict where a share price will go on the basis of its past behaviour. Technical analysts are usually known as 'chartists', for they base most of their research on price charts – pictorial representations of past price movements.

Many City conservatives regard chartists with suspicion –
roughly on a par with astrologers or Tarot card readers. Even so,
it's worth remembering that chartists are only trying to 'read'
the market in terms of supply and demand – the endless battle
between Bulls and Bears. They hope to define trends, when one
or other of these animals is in control, to predict the outcome of
closely matched battles (when many people are buying and
selling at around the same price), and to define points at which
trends might change. Few chartists maintain that their predictions have the force of certainty – merely that there is a greater
or lesser degree of probability that certain price behaviour will
have identifiable consequences.

The whole body of chartist lore requires a separate book –
here it is only possible to glance at some of the more common
and readily understood patterns and techniques. Figure 7
illustrates four of these.

## The flag

This is probably the most common indicator of a 'continuation'
trend – showing that a continued upward movement looks
soundly based. The flag reveals that a strong upward surge has
reached a point where some investors have been tempted to
take profits. This has only a temporary effect on the price,
however, with new Bulls quickly mopping up all stock coming
onto the market. Second time round, the sellers stay their hands
– giving added encouragement to the Bulls. Given that many
'weak' holders are no longer in the shares, the price can be
expected to rise further.

## The double top

This is one of the most common patterns suggesting that a
'reversal' of the price trend is in prospect. In this case, the price
hits a 'top' as profit-takers emerge, and then has another go.
Unconvinced that the price can break past the established
'high', sellers again emerge as soon as that point is regained.
Normally, this will have bearish implications as enthusiasts for
the shares begin to lose confidence. Sometimes, though, the
battle between buyers and sellers can last for some time – the
chart forming triple, or even quadruple tops. The opposite of a

Flag

Double top

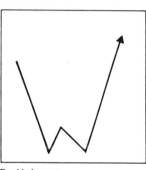

Double bottom

Head and shoulders

*Fig. 7* Chartist patterns.

double top, unsurprisingly enough, is a 'double bottom' with bullish implications.

## The head and shoulders

This is another reversal pattern – one which starts off as a 'flag' but breaks down quite quickly. New buyers find that their numbers are limited, and that a second wave of profit-taking emerges slightly above the old 'high'. On the price's second attempt to break away, many share-holders have become less confident that the price has the strength necessary to enter new ground. When these sell on the first sign of a bounce, it completes the 'head and shoulders' – and generally has bearish implications. Turn the chart upside-down, and you have a bullish 'reverse head and shoulders' pattern.

As well as poring over price patterns, technical analysts also try to establish which shares or sectors are seeing the greatest 'activity' in terms of trading volume, which are 'relatively' strong or weak (compared with the market or sector average), and which are 'overbought' (bearish) or 'oversold' (bullish). All these terms crop up in the financial press, and the newcomer to the stock market will gradually absorb their possible implications for share prices. Charts themselves can be hard for private investors to come by – though again, they are often published in the press for illustrative purposes. It is open to anybody, of course, to plot his own prices on a chart – this can be done either manually, or on one of the many software programs now available to investors with home computers. These are frequently advertised in investment magazines, and in the business pages of the national press.

## FASHION AND SENTIMENT

Fund managers, stockbrokers and other City professionals like to pretend that their analytical expertise governs success or failure on the stock market. Yet, to a far greater extent than most of them would admit (at least to a wider public), investment decisions owe less to cold, logical judgement than to raw emotion. Stock markets are ruled by two dominant sentiments – greed and fear – and few people, however professional, find themselves immune from their influence. Private investors naturally feel excited when they're making money – and distinctly queasy if they're over-committed to a situation which turns sour. But it's worth remembering, too, that most fund managers are now acutely aware of the short-term performance of the money in their care. Failure to keep up with their peers will not just wound their *amour-propre*. In many cases, it may fatally damage their reputations – and even their careers.

When markets are rising strongly, everyone involved tends to feel happy and optimistic – 'good news is good news', as they say, 'and bad news is no news'. As a result, warning signals are often overlooked until they become too pressing to ignore – and then euphoria can quickly give way to panic. That panic itself can easily be overdone. The events of 1974 are just an extreme example – at the height of the crisis, many City folk believed that capitalism in Britain was approaching an apocalyptic end. Two months after the market 'turned' (in January 1975), such absurd fears were already forgotten. It is a general rule that the market's hopes and fears are both prone to exaggeration – sometimes extravagantly so. This is seldom apparent to participants, though everyone is wise enough after the event.

The same comments apply to individual shares and sectors. By the middle of the 1980s, hopes for high-technology companies reached their zenith – analysts projecting magnificent growth rates way into the future. When the industry went into recession in 1985, the entire market was taken by surprise and as usual over-reacted. The very high PE ratios which had predominated in the sector disappeared rapidly, share prices falling virtually across the board. Yet the prospects of some of these companies remained unimpaired – especially those serving specialised 'niche' markets. All that had really changed for them was sentiment. Electronics, hitherto the darling of the stock market, had gone out of investment fashion.

If fashion, greed and fear move prices, so can simple pique. One reason many companies never cut their dividends, even when it would be commercially sensible for them to do so, is that institutional investors might never forgive them. Companies which deliberately or accidentally mislead the market are also likely to be dealt with severely, and neglected for a long time afterwards. Naturally, investors feel very miffed about losing money in such circumstances – and memories in the market are long. Sometimes, companies and their shares are just shunned as pariahs. One obvious example is Lonrho in the 1970s – completely cold-shouldered by the institutions after Edward Heath's famous 'unacceptable face of capitalism' remark. No matter that the yield became extraordinarily high and the PE exceptionally low. For years big City investors just wouldn't touch the shares under any circumstances.

Any private investor who follows the market will soon discover who is the apple of the market's eye, and who is in the doghouse. Sometimes he will feel that these judgements are unfair, even stupid – and sometimes he will be right. For the longer-term investor, it can often pay handsomely to act contrary to accepted market wisdom – 'the crowd', as the cynics say, 'is always wrong'. Maybe. But new investors should be warned that it may take a considerable time for this wrong-headedness to show through. Scoff and sneer at market sentiment if you will, you might as well recognise its power. Sometimes, it just doesn't pay to spit into the wind.

# 8. Examining the quarry

With more than 3,000 companies now quoted on the stock market, any private investor is entitled to feel overwhelmed for choice. In this regard he is no different from the City professionals. To even begin to get to grips with this mass of shares, let alone start making individual investment decisions, it is necessary to break them down into smaller and more comprehensible groups – to 'typify' as much as possible.

It shouldn't be forgotten, even so, that these classifications are merely tools to help the investor find his bearings. Shares do, after all, represent individual businesses – and no two businesses are exactly alike. That said, some of them are at least superficially similar – either in the industries they serve, or in their mode of operation. Looked at from a different angle, companies can also be categorised according to their circumstances. Quite regardless of their business activity, small and rapidly expanding concerns will probably have more in common with each other than with gigantic multinationals – or, for that matter, with other small companies struggling to remain profitable.

## SECTORS

Look at any list of share prices in the papers, and you will find it broken down according to industry. Retailers will be grouped together, as will banks and other financial institutions, oil companies, food manufacturers, investment trusts, property companies and so forth.

Though somewhat crude, these divisions imitate the 'sectors' into which all quoted companies are placed. The *FT* Actuaries' official classification runs to nearly 100 different categories –

many of them, in the press, unceremoniously lumped together as 'Industrials' or 'Miscellaneous'. The official breakdown weights each sector according to the market value of its constituent companies. From these can be produced separate sector indices, and indeed indices of industrial 'groups'. The sector group indices are published daily towards the back of the *Financial Times* (see Fig. 8).

For the larger institutions, with hundreds of millions – even

## FT-ACTUARIES INDICES

**These Indices are the joint compilation of the Financial Times,
the Institute of Actuaries and the Faculty of Actuaries**

| EQUITY GROUPS & SUB-SECTIONS <br> Figures in parentheses show number of stocks per section | Index No. | Day's Change % | Est. Earnings Yield% (Max.) | Gross Div. Yield% (ACT at 29%) | Est. P/E Ratio (Net) | xd adj. 1987 to date | Mon Feb 9 Index No. | Fri Feb 6 Index No. | Thur Feb 5 Index No. | Year ago (approx.) Index No. |
|---|---|---|---|---|---|---|---|---|---|---|
| | | | | Tuesday February 10 1987 | | | | | | |
| 1  CAPITAL GOODS (209) | 799.05 | −1.1 | 7.90 | 3.30 | 16.03 | 0.98 | 807.75 | 798.14 | 785.72 | 627.43 |
| 2  Building Materials (27) | 973.32 | −2.1 | 8.04 | 3.35 | 15.62 | 0.56 | 993.87 | 974.37 | 968.25 | 676.81 |
| 3  Contracting, Construction (28) | 1355.67 | −1.6 | 7.10 | 3.46 | 19.38 | 0.90 | 1377.31 | 1364.23 | 1355.97 | 984.85 |
| 4  Electricals (12) | 1967.91 | +0.3 | 7.66 | 3.99 | 16.76 | 0.44 | 1962.31 | 1966.53 | 1950.59 | 1762.42 |
| 5  Electronics (38) | 1791.69 | −1.1 | 8.02 | 2.30 | 16.53 | 5.85 | 1812.14 | 1810.92 | 1745.83 | 1522.39 |
| 6  Mechanical Engineering (61) | 453.07 | — | 8.87 | 3.67 | 14.39 | 0.58 | 453.00 | 447.34 | 444.76 | 342.59 |
| 8  Metals and Metal Forming (7) | 420.64 | −0.7 | 8.69 | 3.53 | 13.98 | 0.00 | 423.80 | 419.21 | 409.70 | 275.01 |
| 9  Motors (15) | 315.72 | −0.5 | 8.71 | 3.32 | 13.24 | 0.00 | 317.21 | 317.25 | 313.94 | 253.92 |
| 10  Other Industrial Materials (21) | 1350.76 | −1.2 | 6.61 | 4.05 | 18.07 | 0.17 | 1367.47 | 1330.00 | 1313.15 | 1150.57 |
| 21  CONSUMER GROUP (186) | 1072.56 | −1.8 | 6.85 | 2.95 | 18.76 | 1.69 | 1092.15 | 1088.88 | 1070.49 | 806.98 |
| 22  Brewers and Distillers (22) | 1013.13 | −1.7 | 8.40 | 3.42 | 14.95 | 0.00 | 1030.57 | 1019.64 | 1005.75 | 820.82 |
| 25  Food Manufacturing (25) | 819.62 | −1.6 | 8.15 | 3.43 | 16.14 | 1.30 | 832.68 | 834.10 | 817.20 | 586.18 |
| 26  Food Retailing (16) | 2020.94 | −1.1 | 6.65 | 2.69 | 20.88 | 9.56 | 2044.29 | 2039.79 | 1981.11 | 1736.88 |
| 27  Health and Household Products (10) | 1956.93 | −2.1 | 4.86 | 1.94 | 23.88 | 0.02 | 1998.33 | 2012.16 | 2009.31 | 1385.63 |
| 29  Leisure (31) | 1107.60 | −1.3 | 6.78 | 3.75 | 19.35 | 7.39 | 1121.90 | 1123.66 | 1108.62 | 817.33 |
| 31  Packaging & Paper (14) | 577.03 | −0.7 | 6.15 | 2.90 | 21.11 | 0.38 | 581.07 | 578.05 | 572.15 | 409.59 |
| 32  Publishing & Printing (14) | 3393.04 | −0.7 | 5.99 | 3.36 | 21.48 | 3.41 | 3418.63 | 3383.62 | 3333.05 | 2044.24 |
| 34  Stores (37) | 920.23 | −2.7 | 6.97 | 2.94 | 19.50 | 1.24 | 946.17 | 942.26 | 914.90 | 771.34 |
| 35  Textiles (17) | 658.54 | −1.5 | 8.00 | 3.08 | 14.39 | 0.00 | 668.40 | 647.00 | 640.75 | 447.19 |
| 40  OTHER GROUPS (87) | 926.16 | −1.2 | 8.24 | 3.56 | 15.10 | 0.89 | 937.16 | 933.47 | 921.13 | 742.87 |
| 41  Agencies (17) | 1264.35 | −1.7 | 4.53 | 1.72 | 30.04 | 0.45 | 1285.90 | 1270.03 | 1244.23 | 0.0 |
| 42  Chemicals (21) | 1221.76 | −1.7 | 7.27 | 3.45 | 16.76 | 2.85 | 1242.90 | 1241.43 | 1249.51 | 822.59 |
| 43  Conglomerates (13) | 1204.06 | −0.9 | 7.16 | 3.63 | 16.56 | 0.15 | 1215.58 | 1190.35 | 1166.98 | 0.0 |
| 45  Shipping and Transport (10) | 1786.96 | −0.7 | 5.90 | 4.18 | 21.40 | 0.00 | 1799.62 | 1779.38 | 1764.72 | 1461.82 |
| 47  Telephone Networks (2) | 943.79 | −1.1 | 9.91 | 4.08 | 13.76 | 1.09 | 953.85 | 960.70 | 941.66 | 881.51 |
| 48  Miscellaneous (24) | 1237.60 | −0.9 | 9.88 | 3.40 | 11.40 | 0.40 | 1248.55 | 1243.29 | 1219.15 | 910.44 |
| 49  INDUSTRIAL GROUP (482) | 974.66 | −1.4 | 7.50 | 3.21 | 16.91 | 1.29 | 988.93 | 983.50 | 968.20 | 752.53 |
| 51  Oil & Gas (18) | 1637.50 | −2.9 | 10.36 | 5.54 | 12.20 | 0.00 | 1686.91 | 1690.11 | 1661.40 | 1109.20 |
| 59  500 SHARE INDEX (500) | 1030.53 | −1.7 | 7.90 | 3.53 | 16.04 | 1.17 | 1047.88 | 1043.23 | 1026.78 | 783.90 |
| 61  FINANCIAL GROUP (117) | 668.55 | −1.3 | — | 4.21 | — | 0.52 | 677.21 | 666.52 | 654.80 | 543.10 |
| 62  Banks (8) | 741.39 | −1.5 | 17.15 | 4.96 | 8.00 | 0.69 | 752.55 | 741.59 | 719.94 | 537.37 |
| 65  Insurance (Life) (9) | 970.54 | −1.7 | — | 4.90 | — | 0.00 | 987.24 | 955.75 | 930.08 | 821.74 |
| 66  Insurance (Composite) (7) | 514.50 | −2.3 | — | 4.22 | — | 0.00 | 526.48 | 515.59 | 509.09 | 443.25 |
| 67  Insurance (Brokers) (9) | 1181.22 | −1.6 | 8.16 | 4.48 | 15.95 | 1.31 | 1200.90 | 1192.87 | 1186.91 | 1315.27 |
| 68  Merchant Banks (11) | 361.15 | −1.3 | — | 3.19 | — | 0.02 | 365.96 | 366.74 | 369.41 | 313.31 |
| 69  Property (47) | 851.62 | +0.2 | — | 3.45 | 23.22 | 0.42 | 849.81 | 839.09 | 832.37 | 694.89 |
| 70  Other Financial (26) | 411.87 | −0.5 | 7.75 | 3.71 | 16.48 | 1.46 | 414.11 | 410.48 | 405.92 | 301.52 |
| 71  Investment Trusts (96) | 928.45 | −1.2 | — | 2.48 | — | 0.99 | 939.71 | 933.29 | 926.54 | 669.13 |
| 81  Mining Finance (2) | 379.44 | −1.3 | 8.23 | 4.23 | 14.28 | 0.00 | 384.40 | 381.01 | 375.70 | 266.96 |
| 91  Overseas Traders (12) | 841.91 | −0.2 | 9.58 | 5.32 | 12.68 | 0.00 | 844.00 | 837.34 | 832.22 | 630.06 |
| 99  ALL-SHARE INDEX (727) | 932.39 | −1.6 | — | 3.61 | — | 0.98 | 947.20 | 941.18 | 926.51 | 714.06 |

| | Index No. | Day's Change | Day's High | Day's Low | Feb 9 | Feb 6 | Feb 5 | Feb 4 | Feb 3 | Year ago |
|---|---|---|---|---|---|---|---|---|---|---|
| FT-SE 100 SHARE INDEX ♦ | 1874.9 | −35.8 | 1902.1 | 1874.3 | 1910.7 | 1898.4 | 1866.1 | 1846.7 | 1828.6 | 1470.0 |

*Fig. 8* Sectors.

billions – of pounds at their disposal, these sectors are extremely important. With a portfolio so large, it is impossible to invest by selecting the odd company deemed to have outstanding merit. The big funds, in fact, are virtually obliged to have a stake in all sectors of the market, and in almost every company of size. To attempt to 'outperform' the market averages in these circumstances, they can only really tinker round the edges. Accordingly, they break down their holdings according to the official classification, then go 'overweight' (i.e. over-invest) in sectors believed to look promising, and 'underweight' in those which look weak. Within each sector, too, they will stress major companies they like, and underplay (or, if they can, ignore) those they don't. Large funds seldom have the freedom to sell out of any major situation completely – for if they try, they will move the price against themselves on the way down, and find it difficult to re-acquire sufficient stock on the way back up. Naturally, the big institutions do not ignore small companies, indeed most invest in hundreds of them. Nonetheless, the impact each small holding can make on the portfolio at large is usually minute.

Private investors, of course, have no obligation to invest in this way – and should not make any attempt to do so. Given the number of sectors, it is simply not feasible to get a finger in every single pie – if that is considered a desirable aim, it can be better pursued through investment trusts, or large 'general' unit trusts. Moreover, it is usually impossible to use just one 'representative' share as a satisfactory proxy for an entire industrial group. It may work in a few cases (BAT, for example, completely dominates the tobacco sector, and either BP or Shell would do for oils), but in most cases price movements of major companies within sectors vary considerably.

On the whole, it makes more sense to regard share ownership as a way into a particular business, rather than a particular industry, and to regard each company as unique. That is not to say that sectors should be ignored completely – obviously prospects sometimes look particularly bright for certain industries. In addition, because the institutions pay so much attention to them, whole sectors of the market can swing into and out of favour – movements which can affect even the smaller fry. People who concentrate their portfolios in one or two sectors, therefore, are often asking for trouble. For safety's sake, if for no other, it pays to spread your shareholdings around.

# BLUE CHIPS

The term 'blue chip' comes from the casino, where it represents the most valuable gambling counter. In its investment sense, it refers to one of the biggest and most soundly based companies on the market – though there is no precise definition. Household names like British Telecom, British Gas, Marks and Spencer and GEC are all unquestionably blue chips – indeed one would probably have to include all companies classified by The Stock Exchange as 'alphas'. Beyond that, the boundary becomes difficult to draw. Many market men used to claim that any company valued at more than £500m must be a blue chip. After the massive price rises of recent years, £1bn might now be a better cut-off point.

The limit is hardly important. Any company beginning to qualify for blue chip status will be very large, mature, and relatively stable. Table 1 shows the 20 largest companies by market value in the spring of 1987. According to many commentators, blue chips are ideally suited to new investors – for there is no danger of their going bust overnight. In most cases, too, there is little danger of them springing an unpleasant surprise on the stock market. The bulk of stockbrokers' research is lavished on the biggest companies, and most of them have direct contact with the City investment institutions.

The supposed advantages do not end there. Because blue chips are so big, they have a very heavy 'weighting' in the market indices – these are the shares which effectively determine the direction of the market as a whole. Almost by definition, therefore, any reasonable spread of blue chip investments is unlikely to underperform the market by much. If that weren't enough, the biggest companies are easy to follow – for they inevitably attract most comment in the financial press. Moreover, they are exceptionally 'safe' to deal in. Constant two-way business means that the price accurately reflects the state of supply and demand, and the 'spread' between buying and selling prices is generally very low.

These advantages may appear somewhat negative. So, indeed, they are. With a well-spread portfolio of blue chips, you may be unlikely to underperform the market by much – but you are just as unlikely to outperform. Large companies spring pleasant surprises (at least, major ones) on the stock market as seldom as unpleasant ones. And the copious coverage accorded

*Table 1*    The giants of British industry – the 20 largest companies by market value (spring 1987).

| | £m | | £m |
|---|---|---|---|
| British Petroleum | 18541.7 | BTR | 5502.3 |
| British Telecom | 18480.0 | National Westminster Bank | 4754.6 |
| Shell Transport | 14252.4 | Grand Metropolitan | 4403.8 |
| Glaxo Holdings | 11250.7 | Unilever | 4386.5 |
| ICI | 9150.0 | J. Sainsbury | 3984.0 |
| British Gas | 8082.1 | Gresham Group | 3910.2 |
| BAT Industries | 8024.9 | Cable and Wireless | 3889.9 |
| Marks and Spencer | 6666.8 | Barclays | 3654.6 |
| General Electric | 6052.7 | Wellcome | 3556.6 |
| Hanson Trust | 5836.2 | Gt Universal Stores | 3363.2 |

these companies by both stockbrokers and the press means that it is all but impossible to find a situation which the market has overlooked. Minimise the spills of equity investment, and you limit the thrills as well.

Nonetheless, there can be no doubt that most PEP investors, in the early years at least, will be wholly invested in blue chips. Those who opt for the managed schemes will find that the vast majority of fund managers play safe – understandably so, given the limited number of shares they generally choose to administer. Even in most non-discretionary schemes, blue chip investment is the order of the day. Only in the handful offering a choice from between 50 and 100 shares, is the odd smaller company thrown in as a gesture. Until PEP portfolios grow to the point where more latitude is allowed in share selection, it looks as though investors will have little scope to try their hand at the market's 'minnows'.

Prices of blue chips are almost completely determined by the institutions – given the huge turnover of shares in the biggest companies, the small-scale activity of private investors counts for very little. This institutional interest used to argue in favour of their stability, though there's no doubt that blue chips have become more volatile in recent years. To an increasing extent, fund managers' skills are assessed according to their 'performance' against the market indices – performance which appears to be measured over ever-shorter time scales. As a result, they are increasingly inclined to 'top slice' profits (i.e. make partial sales) on leading shares they feel will underperform the market over the next three to six months, and bump up holdings of likely outperformers.

Though these manoeuvres may have very little to do with the long-term prospects of the companies in question, they have a disproportionate impact on share prices. (Only shares which are traded, after all, affect the supply and demand equation.) As a result, movements in blue chips have become rather more exaggerated than hitherto – and are likely to become more so as trading in the largest companies becomes increasingly interna-tionalised. For the unwary private investor, this creates obvious problems. But for anyone prepared to learn how shares behave, it also creates opportunities. Naturally, blue chips (like any other shares) are affected by fundamental changes in the business – profit prospects may improve or worsen, a major acquisition may alter the balance of the company's activities, a large capital-raising exercise may glut the market. Nonetheless you may also be able to spot when a leading share has fallen from grace for no better reason than it is not expected to 'perform' over the following six to twelve months. While institutions focus their attention elsewhere, you may be able to pick up a long-term bargain.

## SMALLER COMPANIES

PEP investors who select one of the few DIY schemes currently available, will probably do so because they insist on investing in smaller companies. In future years, however, this option is likely to become available to larger numbers. As mature PEP portfolios grow in size, and newer investors become more knowledgeable about stock market matters, pressure is bound to grow on most non-discretionary PEP schemes to loosen their current restrictions.

Small companies are both more exciting and more dangerous than large ones. Because few analysts follow them, and even then only intermittently, they have more scope to pull off surprises. If you want to find genuine dark horses on the stock market – excellent companies which are undervalued simply because relatively few investors are aware of their attractions, you will only find them among the smaller fry. It's worth remembering, too, that small companies have far more scope to expand. The ICIs and BPs of this world may grow larger over time, but their scope is obviously limited by the fact that they are already among the largest international players in their respective industries. While companies of this size are never going to double profits in a year, such a feat is quite feasible for minnows earning less than £1m – or even £2m. To succeed spectacularly on the stock market, you really need to follow an unknown company determined to make its name.

Unfortunately, finding the great success stories of tomorrow is a little like looking for a needle in a haystack. Of the 3,000 'gamma' (or third-line) shares quoted on the market, most are pretty mundane. The majority of small companies are going to remain small, even if they manage to soldier on prosperously enough. Their management may lack the ambition or skill required to expand them beyond a certain point, their scope for increasing market share may be limited, the confines of their business niche may be too narrow for outstanding growth. It's worth remembering, too, that if some small companies have greater opportunities than their larger brethren, they often lack their defensive qualities. Over-reliance on a limited range of suppliers and customers can cause problems when business is difficult, and much often hinges on the success of one or two crucial decisions. If a blue chip company launches a major new product which flops, it will simply lick its wounds and bring forward other projects. If the same happens to a very small company, it may cripple the business.

The risks should not be exaggerated – many smaller funds and private investors interested mainly in small companies manage to beat the market average by a wide margin. Nonetheless, it is only sensible to recognise that investment in this area will take you further up the 'risk-reward' scale. A portfolio composed solely, or even mainly, of small companies should be widely spread to minimise individual risks.

## CYCLICAL COMPANIES

Simply put, a cyclical company is one which can expect feast to be followed by famine, and *vice versa*. Most companies, unsurprisingly, participate in the general economic cycle – expanding when demand is buoyant (ultimately from consumers, export customers, or the public purse), and pulling in their horns during a recession.

Naturally, not all companies are affected in the same way or at the same time. If there is a sudden slump in consumer spending, the first impact will be felt among retailers, motor traders, holiday companies and so forth. These will obviously cut back on their own orders to suppliers – but usually not until the trend is well established. In any event, they may have contractual obligations will have to be seen out. Eventually, though, the effect must filter through to the companies supplying goods or services to retailers – and be passed on, in turn, to their own

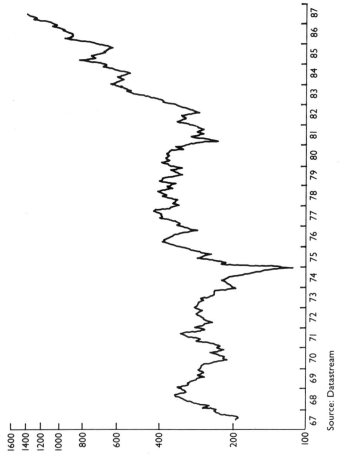

Source: Datastream

*Fig. 9* ICI – a blue-chip cyclical in action.

suppliers of raw materials and capital equipment. This amounts to a gross over-simplification of economic reality – the picture depends on many other important variables like exchange rates, the state of world trade, and levels of government spending. Nonetheless, the general principle holds good. Many industries have their own well-recognised cycles which tend to occur either early or late in the general economic cycle. Figure 9, for example, shows the cyclical pattern for ICI over a 20-year period, as reflected in its share price.

A healthy cyclical company can be expected to do better on each upswing of the economic cycle, and less badly than before on each downswing. Nonetheless, it has to be remembered that the 'depth' of a recession is usually unpredictable (few people expected 1980–81 to be as savage as it turned out), and most investors prefer to play safe. As a result, shares in cyclical companies tend to fall speedily when the economic sky begins clouding over, producing a Bear market. In these circumstances, unless you're taking a very long view, the 'timing' of investment decisions is all-important. The time to get out of cyclicals is usually when the economy is still booming – for the shares will already be high, and the next recession probably closer than most people think. The time to buy, of course, is when everything seems bleakest (if you dare) – for shares will be low and the future more promising than appears immediately apparent. While shares are still falling, you can always switch into cash or move funds abroad. If this isn't possible (and the PEP rules allow only limited scope), one of the best alternatives is to switch into 'growth' stocks.

## GROWTH COMPANIES

Growth companies are those which are still expanding – and doing so virtually regardless of economic conditions. When the economy is booming, many of them can be expected to grow faster than their more mundane cyclical counterparts. But to really qualify for the growth label, they should also be capable of tacking into the wind during a recession.

Growth companies come in all shapes and sizes – though most of them, almost by definition, tend to be relatively youthful. Naturally, too, they tend to be concentrated in growth areas of the economy – at present the electronics, leisure and retailing sectors are particularly fertile territory. It's important to remember, though, that growth companies can crop up almost anywhere – even in traditional industries such as engineering, construction or chemicals. Entrepreneurs are always finding new niche markets to exploit, and some of them are adept at filching market share from older-established and less aggressive rivals.

Essentially, there are two ways of achieving growth – by ploughing a high level of profits back into the business ('organic' or 'internal' growth), and by making acquisitions ('external' growth). Good examples of the former are the blue-chip pharmaceuticals company, Glaxo and the phenomenally successful computers-to-audio equipment group, Amstrad (see Fig. 10). Most growth companies, though, try to speed up their rate of expansion by adding acquisitions – indeed a few make take-overs their *raison d'être*. The trick in this case is to buy up cheaply rated assets and earnings, using highly priced shares as currency. The result, all being well, should be an almost immediate increase in the predator's earnings per share. Best known of the acquisition specialists are Hanson Trust and BTR, though a host of smaller imitators has grown up in recent years. Such companies achieve a disproportionate amount of attention in the press, and are therefore easy to follow.

Growth companies, of whatever stamp, tend to be expensive – apart from the odd exceptional case, their PE ratios will be higher than the market average, and their yields lower. The reason for this is that their long-term prospects should be superior to ordinary, recession-prone companies – and their shares are therefore considered to be worth a 'premium'. The size of that premium depends on two things – how secure the company's growth appears to be, and how fast it is expected to expand. All else being equal, a company increasing profits by 50% a year will have a much higher PE ratio than one expanding at 25%. If it's not exactly twice as high, it will be because the market has serious doubts that 50% growth is sustainable for long.

Because growth company shares are expensive, neither their yield nor asset-backing provide much of a prop if anything goes wrong. We have already seen, when discussing PE ratios, that shares can fall heavily if growth merely fails to come up to exalted expectations. Even more traumatic for share-holders, all

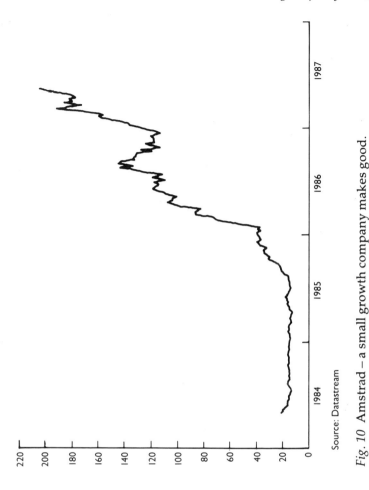

*Fig. 10* Amstrad – a small growth company makes good.

Source: Datastream

growth companies must eventually go 'ex-growth'. The reasons for this can be virtually anything – management may reach the limit of their capabilities, the company may have achieved domination of its business niche, competition may muscle in on the action. Though these events may still lie far in the future (some growth companies stay in an expansion phase for decades), it is essential to watch out for the early signs of creeping arthritis. A share which is being downgraded from 'growth' to 'ordinary' status, however gradually, is most unlikely to prove a rewarding investment.

# SPECIAL SITUATIONS

This group can be divided into numerous subcategories of share, most of which will become rapidly familiar to the new investor if he follows the stock market closely in the press. Here, it is only possible to mention a few :

## Recovery stocks

In a sense, any cyclical company at the bottom of its cycle must be a 'recovery' stock. Normally, however, the term is used mainly in connection with companies which have managed to get into deep trouble through their own mistakes or misfortunes.

Companies in this boat, especially small ones, tend to be written off by the market. As a result, it is often possible to discover very cheap situations where the damage has been put right, and the groundwork laid for a return to prosperity (often this involves new management). Both the risks and rewards of recovery stock investment tend to be high – this area can be dangerous for inexperienced investors. In particular, companies with very high debt levels should be avoided unless you know exactly what you are doing.

## USM shares

Companies quoted on the USM (Unlisted Securities Market) are almost always much younger than those on the main market, and (on the whole) are considerably smaller. The comments above relating to small companies therefore apply, only more so – both the opportunities and the risks are present in exaggerated form. Because of their youth, most USM companies are growth stocks and naturally tend to be concentrated in developing areas of the economy.

## Take-over candidates

As we have already seen when discussing asset backing, some companies are assessed mainly according to their value to a predator. Many others, of course, are liable to be taken over while still perfectly healthy. It is quite possible to predict promising take-over candidates by ferreting through balance sheets, though most investors probably rely on the rumours which constantly arise in the press.

Buying shares for their take-over possibilities is always a bit of a hit-or-miss affair. If the bid emerges, the profit can sometimes be very substantial – particularly if it is vigorously defended, or additional predators enter the fray. On the other hand, the bid may take an awful long time to materialise, if it ever does. Should investors get bored and move elsewhere, the 'bid premium' will evaporate and the shares fall back.

## Predatory companies

Some companies make take-over bids their life's work – boosting their own profits (and earnings) by a succession of clever deals. Companies in this category range from giant blue chips like Hanson Trust and BTR, down to tiny 'shells' (companies with a share quote and little else) used by ambitious but little-known entrepreneurs.

Investment in predators can be treacherous, for they are always dependent on the goodwill of the market. In order to succeed, most predators need their own shares to stand on a very high rating. By issuing these to take-over victims on a lesser rating, they then buy earnings on the cheap. It is essential to remember that the capital base of predators is always expanding as they issue shares. In these circumstances, profits by themselves don't mean much – the crucial yardstick is *always* earnings per share.

## Penny shares

Beginners on the stock market are always fascinated by penny shares – presumably because a share priced at 10p seems much cheaper than one costing 200p. In fact, a price by itself is completely meaningless. If there are 50 million 10p shares in issue, the company concerned will be 'capitalised' at £5m. If it has 2.5m shares in issue priced at 200p, it will also be capitalised at £5m. Apart from the fact that the capital is split into smaller fractions, there is no difference whatsoever. Remember that all important investment yardsticks are reduced to a *per share* basis.

It is true, nonetheless, that many penny shares perform spectacularly on the stock market – but only because they have other qualities. Many of them are recovery stocks with low capitalisations, and are used by entrepreneurs as 'shells' (see above). Then again, so are other small recovery stocks with much higher share prices. Bear in mind that the market-maker's spread on penny shares can sometimes be very steep. The difference between 12p and 14p, for example, is around 15%. If you buy at 14p, you will have to see a rise of that order before you even get back to square one.

# 9. Running a portfolio

Though you will buy shares for their individual prospects, it is important to think of them as a team. Nobody invests in the stock market without making mistakes, or without accidents happening to individual holdings. Accordingly, it is essential to build a 'portfolio' of shares – where the risks (and, be it said, the rewards) will even out. PEP investors who use discretionary schemes can naturally expect their plan managers to look after the problems associated with managing a portfolio. But all non-discretionary plan-holders will have to do so for themselves. At first the scope may (indeed almost certainly will) be rather limited. But anyone planning to open a new PEP each year may soon reach the point where his 'mature' portfolio will be both large and diverse.

## ESTABLISHING AIMS

Many private investors pick up a portfolio almost by accident. They may apply for all the privatisation issues, for example, buy shares (or be given them) in their own company, and have the odd punt on the stock market when they have cash to spare, or when a particular situation tickles their fancy. Yet such a loose collection of shares hardly deserves to be called a portfolio. If you want to invest seriously on the stock market, you must try to establish just what – in aggregate – you are expecting your portfolio to achieve.

The answers will differ according to individual circumstances and predilections. The go-getter may just want maximum growth over an indeterminate time-scale. Somebody planning for a major expense ten years ahead will have a fairly well-defined growth target, and can probably work out what degree of security he wishes to trade for the possibility of additional reward. The man approaching retirement will probably feel obliged to give the safety-factor maximum priority, and adopt a highly conservative investment strategy. Once he's reached retirement (and especially if his share-holdings are held through a PEP scheme), he may want to maximise his portfolio's yield.

There is no need for individual share-holdings to conform to the overall strategy. Somebody wanting a conservative balance between growth and income, for example, might choose to have his entire portfolio in run-of-the-mill blue chips. Then again, he might achieve the same effect by having half his portfolio in very high-yielding shares, half in aggressively-managed growth companies yielding virtually nothing. Obviously the permutations are endless. The point remains, however, that the original objectives of a portfolio should not be forgotten. As some shares rise and others fall, it is all too easy to lose sight of the overall picture.

## BASIC PORTFOLIO MANAGEMENT

The first thing to decide about a portfolio is its ideal size. In the initial stages of PEP investment, this is unlikely to be too much of a problem – most schemes will simply require you to run a 'narrow' portfolio of well under ten shares. As we have seen, eight to ten holdings may be reasonable for anyone anxious to pursue maximum gains and unworried about the risks – he will just have to rely on his good judgement in selecting individual shares. For most people, though, it is too narrow to be anything more than a stop-gap compromise (obviously the effect can be offset to some extent by choosing a scheme with a unit or investment trust option). Later on, when plans have been merged in a mature portfolio, conservatives should hope to have somewhere between 15 and 20 holdings – more than that (even if tolerated by your plan manager) and it may become difficult to follow your portfolio as closely as you should. Obviously these figures are only guidelines. Anyone investing solely in small or semi-speculative companies should normally operate a wider spread than the man sticking religiously to blue chips.

Unfortunately, a portfolio is ever-changing. You cannot just decide on how many shares you want to hold, and what sort of posture you wish to adopt, and leave it at that. Some shares will have to be sold for one reason or another, and new 'unmissable' opportunities will emerge. As some shares do well and others disappoint, your overall investment profile will be continually altering. As market conditions change, you may have to adopt a different strategy for a period. If all these factors weren't enough to contend with, rights issues and take-over bids may distort the picture even more.

Riding this beast can sometimes be tricky. On the one hand, you want to get the most out of individual share-holdings, on the other you want your portfolio to retain some sort of coherence. Striking a balance will always involve compromise – for a portfolio which becomes a strait-jacket can quickly prove counter-productive. The following are just a few hints suggesting how the necessary balance might be struck.

## Running winners and cutting losers

Many people investing on the stock market for the first time make two big mistakes – they take profits too quickly on their successes, and they leave their failures to fester.

When you buy a share, your ambitions for it will normally be pitched pretty high – if it's a blue chip, you will probably be wanting to see a gain of something between a quarter and a third within a year. If it's a small company, you probably chose it because you expect it to double over the same period. Naturally, these are 'best expectations' – you cannot treat such hopes as definite targets. In most cases, assuming a relatively stable market, you will eventually have to settle for less (unless your stock-picking is abnormally good). Nonetheless, you will certainly get nowhere if you snatch every 10% profit as soon as it becomes available. Share prices spend much of their time meandering about in a basically sideways pattern. If they turn into successes, they will suddenly break out of this pattern and 'run'. At the beginning, it is difficult to predict how far they will travel before losing breath – and it is usually best policy just to leave them to get on with it. If you interfere too early, you will ruin any chance of scoring a winner. Such winners are essential in any portfolio, indeed they are the main engines of their growth. Without them there will be nothing to compensate for the also-rans (probably the majority) and the failures.

Shares which turn sour, on the other hand, can be poison. Many people cannot bear to cut a loss, and continue to hold failed shares in the vague hope that they will eventually 'come back'. Occasionally, they might – but it's worth bearing in mind that there's nothing sacred about the price you pay for a share. If you have made a mistake, or something unpredictable has gone wrong with the company, the sooner you face up to the fact the better. Bear in mind that other share-holders will be feeling as worried and uncertain as you are, while new investors are unlikely to fall over each other to buy. Nine times out of ten, those who head for the exits first get the better prices – for a share which starts to fall often develops downward momentum. If you do not cut your losses, you will place your portfolio under a major handicap. Instead of re-investing salvaged funds in new and more promising situations, you will simply end up with an accidental collection of bombed-out recovery stocks. It is often a good test to ask whether, if you didn't already own a failed share, you would be prepared to buy it afresh at the lower price. If the answer is 'no', you should draw the logical conclusion – and buy something else in which you have more confidence.

## Pruning

Running winners is one thing, but it can be taken to excess. Virtually everyone with a well-spread portfolio can expect to have one or two spectacular successes – among smaller companies, it is quite possible for a share to triple or even quadruple within a year. However long it takes, there must come a point where you must take some of those profits – or face the fact that your portfolio will be thrown completely out of balance.

As a simple example, assume you start out with a portfolio of ten share-holdings of equal value. If, at the end of two years, one of those holdings has trebled, while four have risen by 25%, two have fallen by a similar amount, and the rest have done nothing, you will have a quarter of your (considerably enhanced) funds riding on just one share. By the same token, each of your two weakest holdings will account for just 6% of your portfolio. Your 'spread', in other words, will have been significantly reduced – and if you make no changes, the risk attached to your portfolio will rise accordingly.

In these circumstances, even if you think your winner has some mileage left, it is only sensible to consider 'top slicing' some of those profits, and reinvesting the proceeds elsewhere. Naturally, the same goes for cutting losses on the failures, unless you are completely convinced they will recover. It cannot be emphasised too strongly, however, that you should never 'milk winners to subsidise losers'. There is no need for all the holdings in your portfolio to be exactly the same size – you can always afford to let winners run quite far ahead of the pack. Nonetheless, if you never take any remedial action to tidy things up, your portfolio will inevitably go to seed. If that happens, its chances of achieving the aims you've set for it will be much reduced.

## Switching

Most shares in anyone's portfolio tend to be also-rans – they may do reasonably well, moving with the market, but they fail to live up to highest hopes. Some of them may just sit there doing nothing, depressing overall performance, year after year. Sooner or later, impatience will intervene, and you will want to switch. In principle, there is everything to be said for switching – if a share fails to perform, there may well be something wrong with your original buying argument. Even if not, there comes a point when you must admit that few other people in the market are thinking along the same lines. In the meantime, better investment ideas may have occurred to you – and it is silly to turn all of them down because no funds are available. So long as you have shares in your portfolio, funds are *always* available.

Nonetheless, it is a mistake to chop and change too readily. Remember that when you buy a share, it is in the expectation that investors coming after you will be prepared to pay more for it. Your job, in a nutshell, is to anticipate their reasons for paying more – and then get in first. It is simply not reasonable, however, to expect the penny to drop a week or month after you have opened your own position. You may be anticipating bumper profit figures in the next results announcement – but some investors may require hard evidence of those figures before buying. Even then, they may not be satisfied – they may want to see the next set of figures too before convincing themselves of the progress you so correctly foresaw.

The 'timing' of purchases is always a difficult art. Sometimes, if you are lucky, you will see immediate action in the shares – more often you will have to wait awhile for your investment to mature. If you lose patience and switch out of sheer frustration, you run two risks – that your first choice will suddenly take off, and that your second will prove equally mistimed. In addition, of course, you will have incurred a new set of dealing costs – and had to pay the market-maker's turn on prices. On the stock market, Sod's Law should never be underestimated.

Naturally, the above comments assume a basically static or mildly bullish market. On occasions, there can be every justification for making widespread changes to a portfolio. If, for example, you are worried that a Bull market is getting too excited, you may want to take profits on a number of your successful holdings, and switch the proceeds into sectors with defensive qualities. Equally, towards the end of a Bear market, you may decide to switch the emphasis of your portfolio away from growth stocks to cyclicals. No matter how long term your investment aims, there are always horses for courses.

# COMPLICATIONS

Sometimes, new investors notice that share prices seem to change radically without explanation. There are two main causes:

## Scrip issues

As we have already seen, a share price on its own means nothing – it must be related to the number of shares in issue. Sometimes, though, a company (especially a smaller one) dislikes a very high or 'heavy' share price if it thinks it is acting as a psychological deterrent to private investors. To get the price down, it then performs an accounting trick – shifting funds from its reserves into its capital. As it does so, it offers this 'new' capital to its share-holders as a free issue of shares. The result is generally known as a 'scrip issue', though 'capitalisation issue' or 'bonus issue' are synonyms frequently met with.

The effect of a scrip issue is simply to increase the number of shares in issue, and to lower the price *pro rata*. A one-for-two scrip issue, for example, will give you one new share for each two already held – so your holding will increase by 50%. Unfortunately, since the company's profits and assets will now have to be spread amongst a larger number of shares, the market will automatically mark down the price to compensate. In this case, as soon as the additional shares are posted to share-holders, the price will be quoted (ex-scrip) at two-thirds its previous level. If the scrip issue were a one-for-one, share-holders would own double the number of shares at half the price. Nothing, in short, really changes – but it is important to adjust your buying price in line with the scrip to know where you stand. PEP investors will automatically find all these adjustments taken care of when they receive the next statement of their position.

## Rights issues

A rights issue also offers new shares to existing share-holders – though in this case, they have to be paid for. The purpose of the exercise, of course, is to raise new capital for the company. Under Stock Exchange rules, if a company wishes to do this on any scale, it is obliged to offer its share-holders first refusal on the new shares it wishes to issue.

Like scrip issues, rights are offered to share-holders *pro rata*. To take a simple example, you might own 500 shares priced at 100p in a company which offers a 'one-for-five' rights issue at 80p. You are, in other words, being offered 100 shares for £80 on top of your existing holding worth £500. Unfortunately, the 'scrip' element of the offer has to be taken into account – so in reality you are getting no bargain. In this case, the price would automatically fall to 96.67p 'ex-rights' – so if you took up the offer, you would have 600 shares worth £580, not £600.

And if you don't take up the offer? Assuming no price change, you need not lose out – for the difference between your 'rights' at 80p, and the ex-rights price of 96.67p, can be released as cash by selling your entitlement in the market. Essentially, you have three options. You can pay up in full and increase your holding. You can sell your rights in the market and effectively turn part of your holding into cash. Or you can sell sufficient of the rights to take up the remainder – in which case, your position doesn't alter. In practice, almost all PEP managers (even those running non-discretionary schemes) reserve the right to make the decision to avoid undue complications – and most of them will take the third option. If rights issues represent the sort of hassle which puts you off the stock market, this is another area where PEPs can substantially reduce the administrative burden.

# 10. Keeping track

## COMPANY REPORTS AND ACCOUNTS

Except for those investing in schemes confined to unit trusts, all PEP investors will receive copies of company reports and accounts. These are produced after the end of the company's financial year (most commonly 31 March or 31 December), and are generally posted to share-holders a few weeks after the announcement of the year's results. This in turn, is likely to be some six to eight weeks after the year-end – though in a few cases, you may have to wait considerably longer.

Company reports vary considerably in the information they give – some are extremely informative and detailed, others merely conform to the minimum statutory requirements. Study closely a good report, and you will probably be as well (if not better) informed about the current activities of the company as the average fund manager or stockbroker. The main things to look out for are the chairman's statement, the profit and loss account and the balance sheet.

### Chairman's statement

This comes at the front of the report, and usually gives a *resumé* of the previous year's trading, an indication of progress since the year-end, and some idea of how the year as a whole is expected to turn out. Beyond that, it all depends on the chairman. Some are extremely taciturn and unhelpful – they re-state the bald facts, go through the ritual of thanking everyone involved, and reveal that current trading is 'satisfactory'. Others waffle on at great length, giving readers the benefit of their views on anything from government economic policy to the state of the national psyche.

A good chairman's statement will relate the company's trading performance to developments in its own industry and the economy at large, and will go on to report on progress in each area of the business (this last may be found elsewhere as a 'divisional report' or some-such). He will be frank about areas where the company has been experiencing difficulties, and explain what is being done to improve matters. Above all, he will tell you what you really want to know – where the company sees its main opportunities, how it intends to exploit them, and when. Though it's unreasonable to expect too much management information (there are things companies don't want their competitors to know), he may give you the latest state of the order book, and even details of major contracts. Finally, he will tell you how sales and profits have performed in the first few months of the year, and give a good indication about prospects. After you've read a decent statement, you should have a pretty good idea of just where the company is going, (or thinks it is going) and how it intends to get there.

## Profit and loss account

New investors are sometimes intimidated by company accounts, believing them comprehensible only to high-powered accountants. Sometimes, indeed, they are – in which case the average stockbroker or fund manager will be just as mystified as you are. As a rule, though, accounts are accessible enough to anyone of normal intelligence – it's just a matter of coming to grips with the jargon.

The profit and loss (or P&L) account is the formal record of the year's trading. The really important entries are Turnover (or Sales), Pre-tax Profit, and Earnings per Share. Turnover is just the money received by the company for the goods and services it has provided – compared with the previous year, it gives a rough idea how the size of the business has altered. More important is the pre-tax profit figure. To all intents and purposes this is *the* profit figure – and you can usually forget about the others. It shows the surplus left over from sales after deducting the costs of raw materials, salaries, overheads and interest charges – in other words, the money the company has managed to earn for its share-holders and the taxman. Sophisticates will often express profits as a percentage of turnover to produce a *profit margin*. This shows how much profit the company is earning per £1 of turnover, and can be taken as an indication of the profitability and efficiency of the business – the quality, as it were, rather than the quantity. Right at the end comes earnings per share, which we met in Chapter 6. This is simply the company's profit after all deductions (except dividends), divided by the number of shares in issue. Multiply it by the number of shares you own, and you will find out how much the company really earned for you during the year. Normally, you will only see a portion of this in the form of dividends, most of it being re-invested to expand the business.

For the purposes of comparison, all figures in the P&L account are given with the previous year's alongside. Elsewhere, if you are lucky, you will also find a trading record stretching back over five or ten years. This should give you a good picture of how fast the business has been growing, whether it has been vulnerable to setbacks, and if so, how severe or prolonged these have been. On the whole, you will want to find good, regular increases in all the figures – though the emphasis should always be on pre-tax profits and earnings. These are the figures which usually determine share prices.

## The balance sheet

The balance sheet is not a continuous record, merely a statement of the company's finances on the final day of its trading year. By the time you read it, the situation may have altered appreciably – especially if the company's business is highly seasonal. Even so, comparing the figures with the previous year's can still be revealing. Make sure you look at the 'Group' or 'Consolidated' balance sheet. The one which relates to the holding company is of slight importance.

The balance sheet shows two things – where the company's assets are deployed, and where it got the money to pay for them. Assets are either 'fixed' (land and buildings, machinery and other items permanently employed in the business) or 'current'. Current assets are essentially temporary items involved in the company's everyday trading – stocks, bank balances, payments owing (debtors), and suchlike. These are offset by current liabilities – mainly overdrafts, tax due and unpaid bills (creditors). After the deduction of long-term liabilities (usually term loans from banks or HP contracts), we arrive at net assets or share-holders' funds – the theoretical breakup value of the company. Divided by the number of shares in issue, this gives the net asset value (NAV) per share. Multiply the NAV by the number of shares you hold, and the result is what you actually own on the ground.

The second half of the balance sheet shows where the money came from. Called-up capital and the share premium represent funds contributed by shareholders. Capital reserves are usually just accounting items – used to balance any revaluation of property for example. Often the biggest figure will be for revenue reserves (otherwise called retained profits or P&L account). This shows the total of all profits re-invested during the company's life – though other accounting items ('goodwill' on acquisitions, say) may have been written-off against it.

There are three main things to look for in a balance sheet. The first, if you think a company may be a take-over candidate, are assets which may be particularly desirable to a predator – cash and saleable property, for example. Secondly, you may be able to form some impression of how well the business is managed. If current assets are very high, out of all proportion to current liabilities, it may suggest a loose hand on the tiller – those excessive stocks and outstanding bills are probably being financed through a costly overdraft. Thirdly, it's always worth taking a glance at the company's overall debt position (unfortunately, this also means consulting the notes). If overdrafts and loans are very high in relation to share-holders' funds, profits could be clobbered if interest rates rise. Worse still, if business turns down (if there's a recession, for example), the company could find itself in terminal trouble.

You will always be sent reports issued by the companies whose shares you own. But what about those of companies you're just considering? Some non-discretionary PEP managers are prepared to be quite accommodating about providing reports on request – though only if the company concerned is on their list. In any case, there's nothing to stop you procuring a copy yourself from the company's registrars, or consulting a potted version in the Extel card service (see 'Other sources of information' below).

## CIRCULARS

Most discretionary PEP managers provide some sort of back-up information service – though the scope varies immensely. Quite commonly on offer is a six-monthly report similar to those provided by unit trust managers. These will give a brief low-down on prospects for the economy and the stock market, together with an explanation for any changes in the PEP's investments. Given that PEPs are far more narrowly concentrated than unit trusts, it's also reasonable to expect some comment on the prospects for each company held in the plan. Some plan managers, however, intend to go much further – providing explanations after each portfolio change, and general comments about the stock market, individual PEP shares, and other investment matters in monthly or quarterly newsletters. In addition, any plan holding unit trusts must send you a copy of the trust manager's report. If the unit trust is run by a different stable, this may provide a useful 'second opinion'.

Information provided by non-discretionary plan managers also differs hugely. Most of the bigger schemes will provide a potted history of shares on their selection list, together with regular newsletters covering corporate developments and giving reasons for specific investment recommendations. In some cases, these can be quite detailed – culled from research material produced by the manager's stockbroking arm. Overall, though, it's fair to say that the bulk of PEP managers' literature, however frequently provided, is pitched at a fairly low, user-friendly level. For most people, that will be a positive boon. For others, who take a strong interest in stock market matters, its usefulness may be limited.

For the real McCoy, you really want access to stockbrokers' circulars. These range from brief updates on developments, to very substantial studies of market sectors and individual companies. Detailed analytical material of this sort is obviously pitched at City fund managers – and some of it goes over even their heads. Procuring major stockbrokers' circulars is always difficult for the private investor, though some PEP managers are prepared to send plan-holders items of in-house literature on request. They won't publicise the fact – so if you want this sort of service, you should shop around before opening a plan.

If you can't get ready access to brokers' material, it's not the end of the world. Cynics claim that most brokers' circulars are aimed at other brokers' clients – their own institutional customers being tipped off in advance of publication. Certainly, any circular ending up in a private investor's hands (unless he's a client of a small firm specialising in private business) will

usually be pretty stale news – any interesting insights therein
will already have made their impact on the share price. Moreover, while many circulars are extremely informative about a
company's business, there's nothing infallible about their
investment advice. It's not infrequent for one leading City
analyst to conclude a lengthy report with a 'buy' recom-
mendation, while another is saying 'sell' at the same price. A
regular digest of brokers' tips appears in the investment magazine, *Financial Weekly*. If you want to know what the leading
brokers are advising, this can be extremely useful. If you want
to know why (in other than the briefest one-liner terms), it
won't help.

## THE FINANCIAL PRESS

For most people's needs, the financial and investment information readily available through the press is more than adequate.
If you already take one of the quality national dailies or Sunday
'heavies', you will certainly have access to a large City section,
much of it devoted to news and comment about the stock
market and individual companies. In addition, of course, extensive lists of share prices are published every day – so keeping
track of your shares' performance and value seldom poses any
problems.

The doyen of the City Press is the 'pink 'un' – the *Financial
Times*. Few people would buy this as their normal, or only, daily
paper (unless their interest in financial matters had become an
obsession) – but its coverage of economic matters, markets and
company news is unrivalled. At the back of the paper are two
pages of share prices (at least double the space allotted anywhere else), and a host of information relating to unit trusts and
other managed funds, market indices, options and overseas
stock markets. The *FT* is, of course, a working tool for professionals, and as such makes few concessions to accessibility.
Experienced private investors certainly find it useful (much of
the information simply isn't available anywhere else), but the
average beginner is likely to be overwhelmed. Commentary
(especially in the influential 'Lex' column at the back) tends to
be highly sophisticated and somewhat cryptic – and the *FT*
certainly doesn't sully its hands with anything so vulgar as
share-tipping. The Saturday issue is undoubtedly the best

introduction, with substantial reviews of the week's market and company news, and a large section devoted to personal financial matters.

The City sections of the quality dailies are now very substantial, with a large amount of space devoted to stock market news and views. In addition, many of them carry columns discussing at some length the most important company announcements of the previous day – complete, as a rule, with advice for existing or intending share-holders. Until comparatively recently, the *Daily Telegraph* had by far the best and most comprehensive City service, though its rivals (especially *The Times* and the *Independent*) have now caught up. On the whole (bearing in mind that City journalists frequently change jobs), there's little point in changing the reading habits of a lifetime just for the City pages. Note that most qualities expect a reasonable amount of background knowledge from their readers, so novices may still find some of the comment hard-going at first. Much more down-to-earth is the middlebrow *Daily Mail*, which makes share-tipping a speciality and goes out of its way to avoid jargon.

The Sunday papers also have large City sections – some in addition to a separate supplement on personal finance. On the whole, they tend to be more investigative than the dailies, and there is less straight factual reporting. Particularly useful for private investors can be the lengthy company profiles, usually containing an interview with the chairman or managing director, and some comments from City analysts. A feature of all the Sundays is their share-tipping columns. These contain brief snippets of gossip plucked from the City grapevine, and are aimed primarily at people trading short term in shares. If you are fairly active on the stock market, you will almost certainly find the gossip columns interesting – especially if you already own the shares concerned. Nonetheless, they are not a suitable basis for long-term investment decisions, whether you're making your move through a PEP or otherwise.

Among the specialist financial magazines, by far the longest-established is the weekly *Investors Chronicle*, an offshoot of the *FT* but aimed squarely at the private investor. Though the magazine can be quite technical at times, it has made a real effort to become more accessible in recent years. Amongst a traditional diet of company profiles, articles on general investment matters and share-tipping columns, there are now regular features explaining different aspects of stock market investment to novices. Most people, though, probably buy the *IC* for its comprehensive company news service. This comments on the results of almost all listed companies, together with any takeover bids or major deals affecting them, and gives specific share dealing advice in each case. Many enthusiastic investors, who regard the stock market as a hobby, make a point of filing away their copies for reference.

The *IC*'s most direct competitor is probably *Financial Weekly*. While this cannot compare in terms of comprehensive coverage, it does have notable *fortes* like its traded options column and digest of broker's circulars. More recently, a number of monthly investment publications have emerged like *Money Magazine* and *What Investment?* These are usually more wide-ranging than the weeklies, concentrating on general personal finance matters. Nonetheless, they have been increasing their coverage of the stock market as interest has grown more widespread.

## TIPSHEETS

Tipsheets are private investment newsletters, normally sold by subscription only. They can be weekly, fortnightly or monthly, and range from well-presented 8-page documents to glorified scraps of paper run up on a word-processor. As a rule, each issue will contain a leader giving the editor's view of the market, two or three major share recommendations, and a large number of follow-up pieces on previous tips. Some are very chatty and down-to-earth, others assume a reasonably sophisticated audience.

Taken in the round, tipsheets get a very bad press – they are accused of ignorance at best, and of 'ramping' shares for their own benefit at worst. In some cases, these criticisms are justified, in other cases not. Most tipsheet proprietors are not crooks (they do nicely enough out of their subscription income), and some have extensive stock market knowledge and contacts. That said, none of them are as omniscient as they pretend. Those amazing gains shown in the promotional material may be true (sometimes they're tarted up a bit), but they obviously exclude recommendations which proved unsuccessful or turned sour. In reality, you have no idea how the 'average' tip performed.

Does anyone need a tipsheet? If you only intend to invest occasionally, the answer must be no – an annual subscription can cost anything from £25 to £125, and you may never act on the advice you've paid for. For very active investors, the question is rather more open. On the whole, material from your PEP manager or stockbroker, combined with a regular perusal of the City pages (supplemented – if need be – by the *FT* and an investment magazine) should provide more than enough food for thought. On the other hand, if your investment interests are fairly narrow – if, say, you buy only very small companies, penny stocks, or USM shares – it may be worth considering a subscription to one of the specialist newsletters.

Most tipsheets offer a free trial subscription period, so if you must have one it will pay to try out a few alternatives before committing yourself. In this way, you should at least discover whether the sheet deals with the sort of shares you like, whether the editor has a sympathetic investment philosophy, and whether he seems to know what he's talking about. What you should certainly avoid are some of the 'free' newsletters emanating from abroad. Most of these are designed to inveigle you into extremely dubious investments – and some of the firms publishing them are known to be fraudulent.

## OTHER SOURCES OF INFORMATION

Advice on which shares to buy is one thing, but where can you find background material for further research? The most useful sources for private investors are probably the *Hambro Company Guide* and the Extel card service. The former is a weighty and fairly expensive tome, containing a brief anatomy of every company quoted on the stock market. From it you will be able to find the names of the company's advisers, a brief description of its activities, the dates when results are likely to be announced, and an abbreviated record of the past five years' trading. Extel's service is more detailed – it will give a thorough breakdown of both the P&L account and the balance sheet over several years, together with an edited-down version of the latest chairman's statement. Both of these can be found in major libraries, though the Hambro guide may be worth buying if you're an active investor. The full Extel card service is far too expensive and unwieldy for all but the most fanatical enthusiasts, but you can buy individual cards on companies of interest direct from Extel. Alternatively, your stockbroker or PEP manager (if he's particularly obliging) may be prepared to supply you with the odd card on request. If neither of these sources gives you everything you want, it will at least provide you with the name and address of the company's registrars. From these, you can obtain a copy of the latest report and accounts on request.

If you want information on prices, your first port of call will obviously be the morning paper. If that's not recent enough (if, for example, the price is moving very fast day by day) you can always try pestering your broker if you have one – though you won't remain friends if you repeat the trick too often without dealing. Happily, you can now get prices off the TV screen. Prestel gives a lengthy list of share prices, and updates them hourly – though this will probably be of interest only to those already taking the service. A much cheaper alternative is to arm your TV with Teletext. Both BBC's *Ceefax* and Channel Four's *Oracle* give prices for the top 100 companies (and quite a few others which appear to be interesting the market), and update prices roughly once every two hours. In addition, there is a rudimentary market report and company news service, and plenty of additional information concerning currencies, interest rates, overseas stock markets, and other financial matters.

## FINDING YOUR OWN IDEAS

Everyone criticises the tipsheet writers for not publicising their mistakes, but nobody else does either. After you start investing, you'll soon be made aware that all the expertise in the world doesn't stop stockbrokers, fund managers and City journalists from making bad investment decisions, or peddling dud advice. Nobody can say with absolute certainty where a share is going to go next – everything depends on the future state of supply and demand. Analysts can spend weeks producing weighty tomes which give umpteen reasons why a company ought to be re-rated, only to see their efforts entirely wasted. In the end, if the buyers don't turn up in sufficient numbers to overwhelm sellers, the shares won't rise – it's as simple as that. Well argued or not, all predictions about shares are guesses.

In these circumstances, there's plenty of scope for people to back their own hunches. Some of the most successful investors around can't really explain how they operate. They may never listen to anything their broker says, or know how to read a balance sheet – they just keep their eyes open and have a particularly well-developed 'nose' for the market. The only way to acquire this priceless skill is through experience – indeed you may never do so. Some people seem to have a natural talent for spotting winners. Others don't.

If you are just starting out on a stock market career, you have no idea which category you fall into – and of course, you should listen to any advice you can get. Nonetheless, there's no need to be overawed by the experts. You probably know more about the industry you work in than any of them, and can put that knowledge to good use on the stock market. Equally, many City men are not exactly *au fait* with the latest fashions – or with developments on the High Street. Three years ago, for example, any private investor who spotted Amstrad's success in selling computers could have worked out that the company's shares were absurdly cheap. Most institutions were not convinced until, too late, they saw the financial results on paper.

Finally, it should never be forgotten that the City exists in a hot-house atmosphere, where common sense sometimes flies out of the window. At the beginning of 1980, when the price of gold went through the roof, many City men were excitedly punting in gold mines. Meanwhile, round the corner in Hatton Garden, ordinary folk were queuing up to sell their trinkets to the jewellers. In the event, the small men got out at the top, while the experts got their fingers burnt. If that doesn't convince you, just think of the mess the banks got into by over-lending to property developers in the early 1970s, and to third-world governments thereafter. Could you really have done any worse?

PEPs may not be perfect, but at least they represent one more influence encouraging ordinary people to take an interest in their own investments. At present, many people making their debut on the stock market will be as grateful for the helping hand they provide as for the tax breaks. But after a few years have passed – when the tax concessions have started to mean something, and the schemes have become more flexible – it is to be hoped that more and more people will have found the confidence to strike out on their own.

# Glossary

**Account** – Two-week (sometimes three-week) trading period on The Stock Exchange. All transactions completed within an account are settled simultaneously on Settlement Day (second Monday following the account's end).

**All-share Index** – Weighted index of nearly 750 shares traded on The Stock Exchange. Regarded as the most definitive of the various indices, and the one used for most performance comparisons.

**Annual charge** – Annual management fee levied once a PEP has been set up. Charges are either at a flat rate or (more commonly) on a small percentage basis. Normally deducted from dividend income.

**Annual General Meeting (AGM)** – A company's formal annual meeting, attended by the directors and a small minority (usually) of share-holders. PEP investors have a right to attend AGMs, but many plan managers charge heavy arrangement fees.

**Balance sheet** – Formal statement of a company's finances on the last day of its trading year.

**Bargain** – Stock Exchange transaction.

**Bear** – A pessimist, or seller of shares. Hence a falling Bear market.

**Bed and breakfasting** – Selling securities at the end of one tax year, then buying back in the new one. Designed to establish an artificial profit or loss for CGT purposes.

**Bid price** – Market-maker's (or unit trust manager's) buying price. Price available to seller of shares or units.

**Blue chip** – One of the largest 100 or so companies. A relatively stable, safe but unexciting equity investment likely to dominate most PEPs in the early years.

**Bull** – An optimist, or buyer of shares. Hence a rising Bull market.

**Capital Gains Tax (CGT)** – Tax on capital profits arising within a tax year. Currently levied at 30% on gains above £6,700 (1987–88).

**Chart** – Pictorial representation (or graph) of past share price behaviour.

**Chartist** – One who studies charts and price statistics in order to predict future trends in a share's behaviour. Also known as a technical analyst.

**Commission** – Stockbroker's dealing charge.

**Consideration** – Value of a share-dealing transaction before costs.

**Current year** – The first stage of PEP investment. The year during which funds are contributed to a plan.

**Cyclical company** – Company likely to be affected by swings in the economic cycle.

**Dealing costs** – Total cost of buying or selling shares on the stock market, consisting of broker's commission and stamp duty. Most PEP schemes pass these costs on to the investor in addition to management charges.

**Discretionary plan** – A PEP scheme in which all investment decisions are delegated to the plan manager.

**Dividends** – Regular (usually half-yearly) payments made by companies out of profits to their share-holders. Declared on a per share basis and paid net of tax at the basic rate.

**Earnings** – Profits attributable to share-holders after tax and all other deductions (but before dividends). Usually divided by the number of shares in issue and expressed as earnings per share.

**Equity** – see Ordinary share.

**Exempt** – Free of tax.

**Extraordinary General Meeting (EGM)** – Special meeting of a company called in response to a major development.

**FT Ordinary Share index** – An index of 30 leading shares, intended for use as an hourly 'dip-stick' indicator of market movements. Also known as the FT-30.

**Fundamental analysis** – Standard method of assessing shares on the basis of company's earnings, dividends and assets.

**Growth company** – Company still in a secular expansion phase. Often expected to buck any downtrend in the business cycle.

**Holding year** – The second stage of PEP investment. The first full calendar year in which a PEP qualifies for tax relief.

**Initial charge** – Management fee levied on setting up a PEP.

**Institutions** – Managed investment funds – pension funds, insurance companies, unit and investment trusts, etc.

**Investment Trust** – 'Closed-end' managed fund. A quoted investment company exclusively concerned with managing a portfolio of stocks and shares.

**Jobber's turn** – difference between a market-maker's bid and offer prices.

**Market-maker** – A wholesale dealer in securities responsible for 'making' prices.

**Marginal rate** – The highest tax band applying to a taxpayer's income.

**Mature plan** – The third stage of PEP investment – a plan which has qualified for tax relief. Funds can be withdrawn tax-free, or mature plans can be merged in a mature portfolio.

**Net asset value (NAV)** – A company's net assets (share-holders' funds) divided by the number of shares in issue.

**Offer price** – Market-maker's (or unit trust manager's) selling price. Price available to buyer of shares or units.

**Ordinary share** – unit of risk-bearing capital conferring part-ownership of a company. Also called equity.

**Par value** – A share's nominal value. Of little practical significance.

**Price/earnings ratio (PE)** – Share price divided by earnings per share. Normally the most important yardstick used to judge whether a share is cheap or expensive.

**Profit and loss account** – Formal record of a company's trading during its financial year.

**Rights issue** – Offer of new shares pro rata to existing shareholders, usually at a discount to the market price. Otherwise known as a 'cash call'.

**Scrip issue** – An accounting exercise which increases the number of shares in issue. The price will fall to compensate for the extra shares. Also, 'bonus', 'free' or 'capitalisation' issue.

**Stamp duty** – Duty (currently 0.5%) levied on value of share purchases.

**Stocks** – Strictly, fixed-interest securities denominated in units of £100. Now commonly used as a synonym for shares.

**Unit trust** – An 'open-end' managed fund. A vehicle set up to manage a portfolio of stocks and shares, the value being apportioned equally among the units in issue.

**Unlisted Securities Market (USM)** – 'Junior' market in shares which have not yet qualified for a 'full' listing on The Stock Exchange. Shares are traded in the normal way.

**Yield** – Dividends expressed as a percentage of a company's share price. This figure represents the current return on the shares and is comparable with interest rates available on other forms of investment. Yields are always quoted 'gross' – i.e. before deduction of tax.

# Useful addresses

**The Stock Exchange**
London EC2N 1HP (01-588 2355)

**Association of Investment Trust Companies**
6th Floor
Park House
16 Finsbury Circus
London EC2M 7JJ (01-588 5347)

**Unit Trust Association**
16 Finsbury Square
London EC2M 7JP (01-628 0871/0431)

**Securities and Investments Board**
3 Royal Exchange Buildings
London EC3V 3NL (01-283 2474)

**The Securities Association**
The Stock Exchange Building
London EC2N 1EQ (01-588 2355)

**Investment Management Regulatory Organisation**
45 London Wall
London EC2M 5TE (01-256 7261)

**Financial Intermediaries, Manager and Brokers Regulatory Association**
22 Great Tower Street
London EC3R 5AQ (01-929 7211)

**Chase de Vere Ltd**
125 Pall Mall
London SW1 5EA (01-930 7242)

**Extel Statistical Services Ltd**
37–45 Paul Street
London EC2A 4PB (01-253 3400)

**Financial Times**
Market report service (01-246 8026)

# Index

# The Woodhead-Faulkner MoneyGuides

The Share-owner's Guide:
How to invest profitably and safely in shares

J. T. Stafford

Family Finance:
How to make your money go further

Sue Thomas

The Home-owner's Guide:
Buying, building, improving and running your own home

Judith Hargreaves

Personal Equity Plans:
How to build up a nest-egg – with tax relief

John Campbell

Unit Trusts

Sara Williams